ALL
ABOUT
THE
BIBLE

ALL
ABOUT
THE
BIBLE

Compiled by Peter Potter

A
BULL'S-EYE

BOOK

Published by
William Mulvey Inc.
72 Park Street
New Canaan, Conn. 06840

Cover design: Ted Palmer

Library of Congress Cataloging-in-Publication Data

All About The Bible
"A Bull's-eye Book"

1. Bible—Quotations, maxims, etc. I. Potter, Peter,
(Date)   . II. Bible. English. Selections.

BS416.A45   1988   220   86-43157

ISBN 0-934791-06-6

All Scriptural quotations are from the
King James Version of the Bible.
ABS   1967   KJ053-C   Series-D-2

Printed in the United States of America
First Edition

Dedicated to the Clergy.
Men and Women who give their lives
so we can better know Jesus Christ.

Contents

PART I

WHAT THEY SAY ABOUT THE BIBLE

BELIEF

Belief

Within this awful volume lies
The mystery of mysteries!
Happiest they of human race,
To whom God had granted grace
To read, to fear, to hope, to pray,
To lift the latch, and force the way:
And better had they ne'er been born,
Who read to doubt, or read to scorn.

Walter Scott

Take all this book upon reason that you can, and the balance on faith, and you will live and die a happier and better man.

Abraham Lincoln

Faith will totter if the authority of Sacred Scriptures wavers.

St. Augustine of Hippo

Scripture, which proves the truth of its historical statements by the accomplishment of its prophecies, gives no false information.

St. Augustine of Hippo

The Gospels rank among the best attested works of the Graeco-Roman world. They are better attested than the works of Pindar, or Xenophon, or Horace; of Pliny, Polybius, or Suetonius; of Terence or Plautus, Sophocles or Euripedes, or of a score of others, the genuineness and authenticity of whose writings are cheerfully accepted by every classical scholar in the world.

J. P. Arendzen

All human discoveries seem to be made only for the purpose of confirming more and more strongly the truths contained in the Holy Scriptures.

John Herschel

Almost any fool can prove that the Bible ain't so—it takes a wise man to believe it.

Josh Billings

Sir, if the Bible be not true, I am as very a fool and madman as you can conceive; but if it be of God I am sober-minded.

John Wesley

Humanity can never deny the Bible in its heart, without the sacrifice of the best that it contains, faith in unity and hope for justice.

James Darmsteter

Never did there exist a full faith in the Divine Word (by whom light as well as immortality, was brought into the world) which did not expand the intellect, while it purified the heart.

Samuel Taylor Coleridge

━━━━

I believe that the intention of Holy Writ was to persuade men of the truths necessary to salvation: such as neither science nor other means could render credible, but only the voice of the Holy Spririt.

Galileo

━━━━

Scripture does not aim at imparting scientific knowledge, and therefore it demands from men nothing but obedience, and censures obduracy but not ignorance.

Baruch Spinoza

━━━━

For the Bible is not chained in every expression to conditions as strict as those which govern all physical effects; nor is God any less excellently revealed in Nature's actions than in the sacred statements of the Bible.

Galileo

━━━━

God wrote the gospel not in the Bible alone, but on trees, and flowers, and clouds, and stars.

Martin Luther

(Jesus Christ) absolutely trusted the Bible, and though there are in it things inexplicable and intricate that have puzzled me much, I am going to trust the Book, not in a blind sense, but reverently, because of him.

H. C. G. Moule

The Spirit is needed for the understanding of Scripture and every part of Scripture.

Martin Luther

For except a man first believe, that holy scripture is the word of God, and that the word of God is true, how can a man take any comfort of that, that the scripture telleth him therein?

St. Thomas More

When finally the Gospels were written, they did not prove what the Christian believed; they confirmed it.

Fulton J. Sheen

They who have been inwardly taught by the Spirit, feel an entire acquiescence in the scripture.

John Calvin

The Spirit breathes upon the word,
And brings the truth to sight;
Precepts and promises afford
A sanctifying light.

William Cowper

The Scriptures of the Old Israel remained the Scriptures of the "New," for they contained the Revelation of God which He had vindicated and fulfilled. They "testified" of Him.

Gregory Dix

Scripture is full of Christ. From Genesis to Revelation everything breathes of Him, not every letter of every sentence, but the spirit of every chapter.

F. W. Robertson

The central theme of the New Testament . . . is Immortality—not the immortality of anybody and everybody, but of the believer in Christ as risen from the dead. This theme I found everywhere present.

L. P. Jacks

The Bible never commands us to believe, though it commends belief. Such a command would be useless. Belief cannot be coerced.

Morris Joseph

One element the two Testaments have in common. They were established without any abrupt or instantaneous transformation . . . God did not wish us to be coerced, but persuaded.

St. Gregory of Nazianzen

I believe the Bible as it is.

William Jennings Bryan

C

COMFORT

Comfort

If life is pleasant for you and you have no hunger you cannot satisfy, you do not need to read the New Testament. For you will not know what it is talking about.

F. O. Stockwell

The Bible in its various transformations is the great book of consolation for humanity.

Ernest Renan

The book of books, the storehouse and magazine of life and comfort, the Holy Scriptures.

George Herbert

A portable fatherland.

Heinrich Heine

The music of the Gospel leads us home.

Frederick W. Faber

Stars are poor books, and oftentimes do miss: This book of stars lights to eternal bliss.

George Herbert

It is an armoury of light;
Let constant use but keep it bright,
You'll find it yields
To holy hands and humble hearts,
More swords and shields
Than sin hath snares, or hell hath darts.

Richard Crashaw

I'm going to heaven and I believe I'm going by the blood of Christ. That's not popular preaching, but I'll tell you it's all the way through the Bible and I may be the last fellow on earth who preaches it, but I'm going to preach it because it's the only way we're going to get there.

Billy Graham

The gospel is the promise of grace or the forgiveness of sins through Christ.

Philip Melanchthon

If there is anything in this life which sustains a wise man and induces him to maintain his serenity amidst the tribulations and adversities of the world, it is in the first place, I consider, the meditation and knowledge of the Scriptures.

St. Jerome

What are all the Gifts of the Gospel; are they not all mental Gifts? . . . And are not the Gifts of the Spirit Everything to Man?

William Blake

We search the world for truth; we cull
The good, the pure, the beautiful,
From graven stone and written scroll,
From all old flower-fields of the soul;
And, weary seekers of the best,
We come back laden from our quest,
To find that all the sages said
Is in the Book our mothers read.

John Greenleaf Whittier

The Bible is a book in comparison with which all others in my eyes are of minor importance, and which in all my perplexities and distresses has never failed to give me light and strength.

Robert E. Lee

The Old Testament is the story of how God educated mankind to be able to receive the gifts He destined for them.

Jane Danielou

What is a home without a Bible?
'Tis a home where daily bread
For the body is provided,
But the soul is never fed.

C. D. Meigs

Let sleep find you holding your Bible and when your head nods let it be resting on the sacred page.

St. Jerome

In the poorest cottage are Books: is one Book, wherein for several thousands of years the spirit of man has found light, and nourishment, and an interpreting response to whatever is Deepest in him.

Thomas Carlyle

It was a common saying among the Puritans. "Brown Bread and the Gospel is a good fare."

Matthew Henry

How glad the heathen would have been,
That worship idols, wood and stone,
If they the book of God had seen,
Or Jesus and His Gospel know.

Isaac Watts

If you accept this Gospel and become Christ's man, you will stumble on wonder upon wonder, and every wonder true.

Brendan to King Brude

The love that gives, that loves the unlovely and the unlovable, is given a special name in the New Testament, grace.

Oswald C. J. Hoffman

The word "grace" is unquestionably the most significant single word in the Bible.

Ilion T. Jones

The cynic who ignores, ridicules or denies the Bible, spurning its spiritual rewards and aesthetic excitement, contributes to his own moral anemia.

A. M. Sullivan

The glorious Gospel of the grace of God is the profound heritage of the church in its ministry to a lost world.

William E. Gilroy

No poor fellow chained in sin, dead, and bound for hell can every hear anything more comforting and encouraging than this precious and lovely message about Christ.

Martin Luther

It is worthwhile to have a storm of abuse once in a while, for one reason to read the Psalms—they are a radiant field of glory that never shines unless the night shuts in.

Harriet Beecher Stowe

That God is more near, more real and mighty, more full of love, and more ready to help every one of us than any one of us realizes, is the undying message (of the Gospels).

David S. Cairns

Jesus loves me—this I know
For the Bible tells me so.

Susan Warner

G

GUIDANCE

Guidance

A man has found himself when he has found his relation to the rest of the universe, and here is the book in which those relations are set forth.

Woodrow Wilson

A most perfect rule for human life.

St. Benedict

The Bible is the church's charter.

Hugh Pope

A man may learn from his Bible to be a more thorough gentleman than if he had been brought up in all the drawing-rooms in London.

Charles Kingsley

It furnished good Christians an armor for their warfare, a guide for their conduct, a solace in their sorrows, food for their souls.

Gaius Glenn Atkins

The material record of the Bible . . . is no more important to our well being than the history of Europe and America; but the spiritual application bears upon our eternal life.

Mary Baker Eddy

It is the best book that ever was or ever will be known in the world, and because it teaches you the best lessons by which any human creature who tries to be fruitful and faithful to duty can possibly be guided.

Charles Dickens

All human history as described in the Bible, may be summarized in one phrase. God in Search of Man.

Abraham Joshua Heschel

As in Paradise, God walks in the Holy Scriptures, seeking man.

Ambrose of Milan

The Bible nowhere calls upon men to go out in search of peace of mind. It does call upon men to go out in search of God and the things of God.

Abba Hillel

The Holy Ghost is certainly the best preacher in the world, and the words of Scripture the best sermons.

Jeremy Taylor

Holy Scripture contains all things necessary to salvation; so that whatsoever is not read therein nor may be proved thereby, is not to be required of any man that it should be believed as an article of faith, or be thought requisite or necessary to salvation.

Doctrine and Discipline of
the Methodist Church, 1952

The only objection against the Bible is a bad life.

The Earl of Rochester

And what is the Bible after all but the history of a deliverer; of God proclaiming himself as man's deliverer from the state into which he is ever ready to sink,—a state of slavery to systems, superstitions, the world, himself, atheism?

Frederick D. Maurice

The discipline of the Old Testament may be summed up as a discipline teaching us to abhor and flee from sin.

Matthew Arnold

The Scriptures inculcate chiefly the necessity of repairing what was lost by sin and of reconstructing the broken order of things.

St. Bonaventure

The importance of secular history decreases in direct proportion of the intensity of man's concern with God and himself. . . . The message of the New Testament is not an appeal to historical action but to repentance.

Karl Lowith

―――――

The fundamental conviction of the prophets . . . was the conviction that God demands righteousness and demands nothing but righteousness.

Walter Rauschenbusch

―――――

We need never tremble for the Word of God, thought we may tremble at it and the demands which it makes upon our faith and courage.

William Robertson Smith

―――――

These words give us all a sure medicine . . . by which we shall keep from sickness, not the body . . . but the soul, which here preserved from the sickness of sin, shall after this eternally live in joy.

St. Thomas More

―――――

Of the whole of Scripture there are two parts: the law and the gospel. The law indicates the sickness, the gospel the remedy.

Philip Melanchthon

You venture to judge the Bible and up to a point it submits to your judgment, and then you may find the roles reversed— and you are in the dock and the Bible is the judge pronouncing sentence upon you.

A. C. Craig

The New Testament, and to a very large extent the Old, is the soul of man. You cannot criticize it. It criticizes you.

John Jay Chapman

It is only if we as Christians can view ourselves as the sort of people who crucified Christ that the New Testament can have any saving effect upon us.

James A. Pike

For saving and perfecting of ourselves and of others there is at hand the very best of help in the Holy Scriptures, as the Book of Psalms, among others, so contantly insists.

Pope Leo XIII

The best gift God has given to man. . . . But for it we could not know right from wrong.

Abraham Lincoln

I have made a covenant with my Lord God that He send me neither visions nor dreams, nor even angels. For I am well satisfied with the gift of Holy Scriptures, which gives me abundant instruction and all that I need to know both for this life and for that which is to come.

Martin Luther

The Bible is God's chart for you to steer by, to keep you from the bottom of the sea; and to show you where the harbor is, and how to reach it without running on rocks or bars.

Henry Ward Beecher

If we abide by the principles taught by the Bible, our country will go on prospering.

Daniel Webster

Nobody ever outgrows Scripture; the book widens and deepens with our years.

Charles Haddon Spurgeon

Dear Lord, this Book of thine
Informs me where to go,
For grace to pardon all my sin,
And make me holy too.

Isaac Watts

The Sacred Books were not given to men by God to satisfy their curiosity or to provide them with material for study and research, but, as the Apostle observes, in order that these Divine Words might "instruct in justice, by the faith which is in Christ Jesus," and "that the man of God may be perfect, equipped for every good work."

Pope Pius XII

God's Word is not simply a communication or an objective statement, but a positive command which does not permit man to assume the attitude of a spectator or to enjoy mere disinterested research.

Adolph Keller

Jest not with the two-edged sword of God's word.

Thomas Fuller

It is not enough, according to the New Testament, for men simply to treat each other justly. They are also under the seemingly impossible requirement to love each other. . . . This is the biblical call for neighborliness, which is a great deal more than mere justice.

James Sellers

The Bible tells us to love our neighbors, and also to love our enemies; probably because they are generally the same people.

Gilbert K. Chesterton

The Scriptures teach us the best way of living, the noblest way of suffering, and the most comfortable way of dying.

John Flavel

A book that sweats people into unity.

Leon Feuchtwanger

Lord, Thy word abideth,
And our footsteps guideth;
Who its truth believeth
Light and joy receiveth.

Henry Williams Baker

The Bible is the Book that holds hearts up to the light as if held against the sun.

William A. Quayle

1

INFLUENCE

INSPIRATION

INTERPRETATION

Influence

Western civilization is founded upon the Bible; our ideas, our wisdom, our philosophy, our literature, our art, our ideals come more from the Bible than from all other books put together. It is a revelation of divinity and of humanity.

William Lyon Phelps

Even those who do not believe that the Bible is the revelation of God, will admit that it is the supreme revelation of man.

William Lyon Phelps

The Bible speaks primarily to the Church, but it also speaks through the Church to the world inasmuch as the whole world is claimed by the Church's Lord.

Alan Richardson and W. Schweitzer

The whole of morality is based on the Bible; there is not a principle, however resolutely secular it would like to be, that did not originate, often receive its final formulation, too, in Scripture.

Henri Daniel-Rops

The Sun of the Bible penetrates into the proudest palaces and the humblest shanties; . . . the Sun of the Bible radiates warmth and strength, and has called into being a system of morality which has become the corner-stone of human civilization.

I. Friedlander

So long as tens of thousands of Bibles are printed every year, and circulated over the whole habitable globe, and the masses in all English-speaking nations revere it as the word of God, it is vain to belittle its influence.

Elizabeth Cady Stanton

The Bible is an inexhaustible fountain of all truths. The existence of the Bible is the greatest blessing which humanity ever experienced.

Immanuel Kant

The soul can do without everything, except the word of God, without which none of all of its wants are provided for.

Martin Luther

Wherever the Gospel is preached, no matter how crudely, there are bound to be results.

Billy Graham

In the beginning, we had the land and the white man had the Bible. Then we had the Bible and the white man had the land.

African saying

No individual, no Caesar or Napoleon, has had such a part in the world's history as this book. . . . If only shards and broken pieces of our civilization should remain, among them would still be found the Bible, whole and uninjured. The book that outlived the Roman Empire will outlive any destruction that impends.

E. S. Bates

England has two books: the Bible and Shakespeare. England made Shakespeare but the Bible made England.

Victor Hugo

When in 1796 Bishop Richard Watson published "An Apology for the Bible", George III commented: "Apology for the Bible! Apology for the Bible! I did not know that the Bible required an apology."

Alan Richardson

We present you with this book, the most valuable thing that this world affords. Here is wisdom, this is the Royal Law: these are the lively oracles of God.

Coronation Service

All the good from the Savior of the world is communicated through this Book. All the things desirable to man are contained in it.

Abraham Lincoln

I believe today's young people will discover that people, even the best people, are not gods. They will then recover the Bible. They will see it as a book which, far from merely supporting the "establishment," brings all human contrivance under judgment. They will see it as a book whose author loves people enough to tell the truth about them. They may even, as the book begins to speak to them, hear a word from beyond the book and a voice they did not expect to hear.

Karl A. Olsson

The Bible is a book of faith, and a book of doctrine, and a book of morals, and a book of religion, of special revelation from God; but it is also a book which teaches man his own individual responsibility, his own dignity, and his equality with his fellow-man.

Daniel Webster

Actually, there is power in the Gospel for those who know how to receive it. The three letters TNT, abbreviation for The New Testament, on the back of some small editions of this book, cryptically suggest this fact!

G. Ray Jordan

Bible history is focused history. The forwardness climbs to a lighted hilltop, and all history beyond that point is in that light, moving on to the fulfillment of the light. The focal point in Christ; and the lighted hilltop, though the light is darkness, is Calvary.

George A. Buttrick

Christ is the Master; the Scriptures are only the servant. The true way to test all the Books is to see whether they work the will of Christ or not. No Book which does not preach Christ can be apostolic, though Peter or Paul were its author. And no Book which does preach Christ can fail to be apostolic, though Judas, Ananias, Pilate or Herod were its author.

Martin Luther

The Bible, the greatest medicine chest of humanity.

Heinrich Heine

Any individual or institution that could take the Bible to every home in this country would do more for the country than all the armies from the beginning of our history to the present time.

David J. Brewer

It is the glory of the Gospel charter and the Christian constitution, that its author and head is the Spirit of truth, essential reason as well as absolute and incomprehensible Will.

Samuel Taylor Coleridge

The Old Testament differs from the Scriptures of other religions in that it proclaims a God whose righteous will is the norm of history and of individual lives.

Sydney Cave

It is the very marrow of a race of lions. Stout hearts are those that feed on it. Without the antidote of the Old Testament the Gospel is tasteless and unwholesome fare. The Bible is the bone and sinew of nations with the will to live.

Romain Rolland

Our Jewish Bible has implanted itself in the table-talk and household life of every man and woman in the European and American nations.

Harry Emerson Fosdick

It is precisely in the Old Testament that is reached the highest ethical note ever yet sounded . . . by man.

Israel Zongwill

By the Mosaic Law men may be said to be purified, and by the prophetic revelations they are enlightened, and by the evangelical message they are brought to perfection.

St. Bonaventure

The church as a whole must be concerned with both evangelism and social action. It is not a case of either-or; it is both-and. Anything less is only a partial Gospel, not the whole counsel of God.

Robert D. de Haan

What a book! great and wide as the world, rooted in the abysmal depths of creation and rising aloft into the blue mysteries of heaven . . . . Sunrise and sunset, promise and fulfillment, birth and death, the whole human drama, everything is in this book. . . . It is the book of books, Biblia.

Heinrich Heine

What the Bible affirms is not the primacy of the spiritual over the material, or the power of ideals in history, but the rule of God over all.

Paul Ramsey

Lo, here a little volume, but great book!
(Fear it not, sweet, It is no hypocrite),
Much larger in itself than in its look.

Richard Crashaw

A glory gilds the sacred page,
Majestic like the sun,
It gives a light to ev'ry age,
It gives, but borrows none.

William Cowper

Inspiration

It teaches us to see, feel, grasp, and comprehend faith, hope, and charity far otherwise than mere human reason can; and when evil oppresses us it teaches how these virtues throw light upon the darkness, and how, after this poor miserable existence of ours on earth, there is another and eternal life.

Martin Luther

Its object is not to convince the reason, but to attract and lay hold of the imagination.

Baruch Spinoza

You will feel yourself breathed upon by divine will, affected, seized, transfigured, in an ineffable manner, if you approach Scripture religiously with veneration, humbly.

Desiderius Erasmus

When you have read the Bible, you will know it is the word of God, because you will have found it the key to your own heart, your own happiness and your own duty.

Woodrow Wilson

I recite the creeds, and wonder and doubt. And then I read in the Gospels, and out of some sentence or some act . . . springs a flash of light, comes a sudden lifting of the curtain, which compels me to say: This thing is of man and more than man.

Paul Elmer More

The words of the Bible find me at greater depths of my being than any other book does. Whatever finds me brings with it an irresistible evidence of having proceeded from the Holy Spirit.

Samuel Taylor Coleridge

Israel's Sacred Books stand so happily combined together, that, even out of the most diverse elements, the feeling of a whole still rises before us. They are complete enough to satisfy, fragmentary enough to excite, barbarous enough to rouse, tender enough to appease.

Johann W. von Goethe

By the reading of Scripture I am so renewed that all nature seems renewed around me and with me. The sky seems to be a pure, a cooler blue, the trees a deeper green, light is sharper on the outlines of the forest and the hills and the whole world is charged with the glory of God and I feel fire and music in the earth under my feet.

Thomas Merton

Reading the New Testament is the discovery of a new path of human understanding by the flares that burned on the heights of Golgotha. . . . Out of the New Testament came a definition of divine love that has lit the tapers of faith and hope in the hearts of the world.

A. M. Sullivan

It is when we think of the Bible in terms of Christ that we best understand what it is and what it is not.

John J. Wright

A man who loves his wife will love her letters and her photographs because they speak to him of her. So if we love the Lord Jesus we shall love the Bible because it speaks to us of him.

John R. W. Scott

I did not go through the Book. The Book went through me.

A. W. Tozer

What Dryden said about Chaucer applies in infinitely greater degree to the Bible: "Here is God's plenty."

Robert J. McCracken

The word joy is found 164 times in a concordance of the Bible, and the word rejoice is repeated 191 times. Truly the Bible is a book of joy and gladness because it is a record of God's relationships with man and of man's continuous search for communion and fellowship.

Kirby Page

───

Holy Scripture is so exalted that there is no one in the world . . . wise enough to understand it so fully that his intellect is not overcome by it. Nevertheless, man can stammer something about it.

Blessed Angela of Foligno

───

For the people who know the Bible and Tradition and the complete history of humanity, Joy is the most infallible sign of the presence of God.

Leon Bloy

───

The New Testament is the most joyful book in the world. It opens with joy over the birth of Jesus, and it ends with a superb picture of a multitude which no man could number, singing Hallelujah Choruses.

Harry Emerson Fosdick

───

When I open and turn over with reverent joy the leaves of the Gospels, I feel that here is enshrined the highest achievement of Man the Artist, a creation to which nothing can be added, from which nothing can be taken away.

Havelock Ellis

Southern culture has fostered a type of imagination that has been influenced by Christianity of a not too unorthodox kind and by a strong devotion to the Bible, which has kept our minds attached to the concrete and the living symbol.

Flannery O'Connor

━━━

People who win (the Nobel Prize) always seem to have to write the Old and New Testaments to show how great they are. They forget that these were written well enough in the first place.

Ernest Hemingway

━━━

The history of every individual man should be a Bible.

Novalis

━━━

The Christian message was not Good Advice; it was News, Good News of God.

Sydney Cave

━━━

When, in obedience, we all get back to find again the Gospel principles of fellowship and worship that are never old, the temper of our respective zeals will rise again to white heat.

George F. MacLeod

What built St. Paul's Cathedral? Look at the heart of the matter, it was that divine Hebrew Book,—the word partly of the man Moses, an outlaw tending his Midianitish herds, four thousand years ago, in the wildernesses of Sinai! It is the strangest of things, yet nothing is truer.

Thomas Carlyle

———

We advise all who feel hemmed in by a closed and stifling world to open the Old and New Testaments. They will there find vistas, which will liberate them, and the excellent food of the only true God.

Emmanuel Suhard

———

When the doctrine of the Gospel becomes the reason of our mind, it will become the principle of our life.

Benjamin Whichcote

———

The Bible is an inexhaustible fountain of all truths. The existence of the Bible is the greatest blessing which humanity ever experienced.

Immanuel Kant

———

The stars, that in their courses roll,
Have much instruction given;
But thy good Word informs my soul
How I may climb to heaven.

Isaac Watts

Other books were given for our information, the Bible was given for our transformation.

Anonymous

Interpretation

Holy Scripture is the unchangeable word of God to which man must bend himself, and not something which he can bend to his own personal ideas.

Jean Danielou

You who believe what you like of the gospels and believe not what you like, believe yourselves rather than the gospel.

St. Augustine of Hippo

Wrestle with no such texts as might bring us in a doubt and perplexity of any of those articles wherein every good Christian man is clear.

St. Thomas More

The Gospel is so welded together in truth, that if one part or article is renounced, the rest is at once deprived of meaning.

Beded Jarrett

The interpreter should not be a lover of contention; but possess meekness in his pity.

St. Augustine of Hippo

If the Spirit of God has really wrought in the production of this Book (the Bible) from start to finish, it is hard to conceive of error save such as may have crept into the text in the course of transmission. . . . We have no reason to conclude from the data of textual criticism that the writers of Scripture were so left to their own devices that error should be expected in the autographs.

Everett F. Harrison

Is there any reason that we, who have not heard Christ speak, should have a clearer apprehension of the meaning of His recorded discourses on a given point, than the Apostles who did?

John Henry Newman

The more we convince ourselves of the liability of the New Testament writers to mistake, the more we really bring out the greatness and worth of the New Testaments. . . . The New Testament exists to reveal Jesus Christ, not to establish the immunity of its writers from error.

Matthew Arnold

In their eyes a profane book or ancient document is accepted without hesitation, whilst the Scripture, if they only find in it a suspicion of error, is set down with the slightest possible discussion as quite untrustworthy.

Pope Leo XIII

It will never be lawful to restrict inspiration merely to certain portions of the Holy Scriptures, or to grant that the sacred writers could have made mistakes. . . . They render in exact language, with infallible truth, all that God commanded, and nothing else.

Pope Leo XIII

═══════

If in these books I meet anything which seems contrary to truth I shall not hesitate to conclude that the text is faulty, or that the translator has not expressed the meaning of that passage, or that I myself do not understand.

St. Augustine of Hippo

═══════

He is mistaken, who gives the Scripture a meaning, however truthful or however edifying, which was not intended by the sacred author.

St. Augustine of Hippo

═══════

The testimony of Scripture . . . is plain and intelligible, when we are content to accept it as a fact for our practical guidance; it becomes incomprehensible only when we attempt to explain it as a theory capable of speculative analysis.

Dean Mansel

═══════

We must be on guard against giving interpretations of Scripture that are farfetched or opposed to science, and so exposing the word of God to the ridicule of unbelievers.

St. Augustine of Hippo

In expounding the Bible, if one were always to confine one-
self to the unadorned grammatical meaning, one might fall
into error. Not only contradictions, and propositions far from
true might thus be made to appear in the Bible, but even
grave heresies and follies. . . . For that reason . . . nothing
physical which sense-experience . . . proves to us ought to be
called in question (much less condemned) upon the testimony of biblical passages which may have some different
meaning beneath the words.

Galileo

For neither the prophets nor the Savior Himself announced
the divine mysteries so simply as to be easily comprehended
by all persons whatever . . . . All things are right to them that
understand, says the Scripture: to those, that is, who per-
fectly preserve His revealed interpretations of the Scriptures,
according to the Church's rule.

St. Clement of Alexandria

All Scripture was written primarily for an entire people, and
secondarily for the whole human race; consequently its contents must necessarily be adapted, as far as possible, to the
understanding of the masses.

Baruch Spinoza

The Bible is not the sole basis of our religion, for in addition
to it we have two other bases. One of these is anterior to it:
namely, the fountain of reason. The second is posterior to it:
namely the source of tradition. Whatever, therefore, we may
not find in the Bible, we can find in the two other sources.

Saadia Ben Joseph

Owing to the very depth of Holy Scripture itself, all do not receive it in one and the same sense; but one in one way and another in another interpret the declarations of the same writer, so that it seems possible to elicit it as many opinions as there are men.

St. Vincent of Lerins

The entire book of the Scriptures has been reoriented and reinterpreted. It becomes a new book. To the person who has been through this process of research the Bible emerges as a much greater book.

Rufus M. Jones

Notice that the structure and style of Scripture is a structure so unsystematic and various, and a style so figurative and indirect, that no one would presume at first sight to say what is in it and what is not.

John Henry Newman

We ought to listen to the Scriptures with the greatest caution, for as far as understanding of them goes we are as but little children.

St. Augustine of Hippo

High among of the devil's preferences in Holy Writ must be the verses that can be perversely warped out of their real meaning to make nice booby traps. Here is a beauty: "For ye have the poor always with you."

Halford E. Luccock

On any of the secret mysteries of the Scripture, we ought to philosophize with great sobriety and moderation; and also with extreme caution, lest either our ideas of our language should proceed beyond the limits of the divine word.

John Calvin

We are not left at liberty to pick and choose out of its contents according to our judgment, but must receive it all, as we find it, if we accept it at all.

John Henry Newman

The minister who is a faithful interpreter of the Word continues to exercise considerable authority because of the actual power of the Bible.

H. Richard Niebuhr

It is one of the glories of the Bible that it can enshrine many meanings in a single passage . . . . Each man marvels to find in the divine Scriptures truths which he has himself thought out.

St. Thomas Aquinas

The Holy Bible is an abyss. It is impossible to explain how profound it is, impossible to explain how simple it is.

Ernest Hello

Private interpretation meant that any group of men, however ignorant, need only to be able to read the Bible to be in possession of the ultimate, undeniable truth about almost any important question of human life.

Everett Dean Martin

What God has so plainly declared to the world is in some parts of Scripture stated in plain words, while in other parts it still lies hidden under obscure words.

Martin Luther

The Scriptures, though not everywhere
Free from corruption, or entire, or clear,
Are uncorrupt, sufficient, clear, entire
In all things which our needful faith require.

John Dryden

We ought, indeed, to expect occasional obscurity in such a book as the Bible, . . . but God's wisdom is a pledge that whatever is necessary for us, and necessary for salvation, is revealed too plainly to be mistaken.

William Ellery Channing

No one should be so presumptuous as to think that he understands the whole of Scripture.

Pope Leo XIII

Sometimes, when I read spiritual treatises . . . my poor little mind grows weary, I close the learned book, . . . and I take the Holy Scriptures. Then all seems luminous, a single word opens up infinite horizons to my soul, perfection seems easy.

St. Teresa of Lisieux

Such as it is, the Gospel is enough for me. As soon as I face it again, everything again becomes luminous for me. Man's explanation only darkens it.

André Gide

The sacred book no longer suffers wrong, Bound in the fetters of an unknown tongue, But speaks with plainness art could never mend, What simplest minds can soonest comprehend.

William Cowper

No matter how many new translations of the Bible come out, the people still sin the same way.

Anonymous

Although we may differ in the manner in which tradition, reason and natural law may be used in the interpretation of Scripture, any teaching that clearly contradicts the Biblical positions cannot be accepted as Christian.

Alan Richardson and W. Schweitzer

51

If a theologian does not want to err, he must have all Scripture before his eyes, must compare apparently contradictory passages and, like the two cherubim facing each other from opposite sides, must find the agreement of the difference in the middle of the mercy seat.

Martin Luther

There can be no falsehood anywhere in the literal sense of Holy Scripture.

St. Thomas Aquinas

The Old Testament cannot be understood without the New, which comes to fulfill, to justify and explain.

Paul Claudel

We believe that God never contradicts in one part of Scripture what He teaches in another; and never contradicts in revelation what He teaches in His works and providence.

William Ellery Channing

We acknowledge only that interpretation as true and correct which is fairly derived from the spirit and language of the Scriptures themselves, in accordance with the circumstances and in harmony with other and plainer passages.

Henry Bullinger

The fundamental attitude of mind in Scripture—aspiration towards God, love reaching out to Him, the ardent desire one day to possess Him—is the only thing which can enable us to penetrate its mystery.

Henri Daniel-Rops

Explain the Scriptures by the Scriptures.

St. Clement of Alexandria

The gospel is a declaration, not a debate.

James S. Stewart

I hear the objection: "What need is there for interpretation when Scripture is entirely clear?" But if it is so clear, why have such eminent men groped so blindly and for so many centuries in such an important matter?

Desiderius Erasmus

He who cultivates only one precept of the Gospel to the exclusion of the rest in reality attends to no part at all.

John Henry Newman

The Bible is a harp with a thousand strings. Play on one to the exclusion of its relationship to the others, and you will develop discord. Play on all of them, keeping them in their places in the divine scale, and you will hear heavenly music all the time.

William P. White

LITERATURE

Literature

A collection of literature, containing in a pre-eminent measure the growth of the consciousness of God in the human soul, as interpreted by the pre-eminent religious leaders of a pre-eminently religious people.

Lyman Abbott

The English Bible is the first of our national treasures.

King George V

What the Christian religion is has been laid down once and for all by the founder of the religion in words that can be read by all in a translation of singular beauty.

Virginia Woolf

The Bible is like an old Cremona; it has been played upon by the devotion of thousands of years until every word and particle is public and tunable.

Desiderius Erasmus

The Bible as we now read it in the Authorized Version has had, and will continue to have, more influence upon the English language and upon English prose style than any other book.

R. W. Chambers

Great consequences have flowed from the fact that the first truly popular literature in England—the first which stirred the hearts of all classes of people . . . was the literature comprised within the Bible.

John Fiske

The English Bible is a book which, if everything else in our language should perish, would alone suffice to show the whole extent of its beauty and power.

Thomas B. Macaulay

The poetry of the Bible is not only the most wonderful kind, but it is God's literature.

Hugh Pope

There are no words in the world more knowing, more disclosing and more indispensable, words both stern and graceful, heartrending and healing.

Abraham Joshua Heschel

There are no songs comparable to the songs of Zion; no orations equal to those of the prophets; no politics like those which the Scriptures teach.

John Milton

How many times one has laid the Bible aside in favor of what seemed more real and compelling . . . only to be driven back to it again by the great hunger to let the measured dignity and beauty of its language stir in him an emotion like that which comes in listening to classical music or in seeing a finely proportioned building.

Douglas V. Steere

Consider the gentleness of Jesus, the purity of His morals, the persuasiveness of His teaching. How lofty His principles! What wisdom in His Words! How opportune, frank and direct His answer! How can the Gospel history be an invention?

Jean Jacques Rousseau

The most stupendous book, the most sublime literature, even apart from its sacred character, in the history of the world.

Blanche Mary Kelly

No man ever did or ever will become truly eloquent without being a constant reader of the Bible, and an admirer of the purity and sublimity of its language.

Fisher Ames

A person who professes to be a critic in the delicacies of the English language ought to have the Bible at his fingers' ends.

Thomas B. Macaulay

The Old Testament and the New are imperishable master-pieces of literature largely because they speak frankly and powerfully the facts of life.

James M. Gillis

—————

Intense study of the Bible will keep any writer from being vulgar in point of style.

Samuel Taylor Coleridge

—————

The Bible is not only the foundation of modern English literature, it is the foundation of Anglo-Saxon civilization.

William Lyon Phelps

—————

The Bible is the most thought-suggesting book in the world. No other deals with such grand themes.

Herrick Johnson

—————

The Bible is a postgraduate course in the richest library of human experience.

Herbert Hoover

—————

The Bible is a page torn out of the great volume of human life; only, torn by the hand of God, and annotated by his Spirit.

Joseph Parker

The Bible makes an extraordinary impression on the historian . . . its concrete shape shrouded from the outset in the loftiest beliefs; then its stately expansion, its confident though hidden progress to a boundless and unpredictable end: nowhere else can be found anything in the least like it.

Henry de Lubac

The literature of a great race, the literature of a great movement toward realizing the relation of God to man.

George P. Atwater

The Bible is interested in what has happened in the world in so far as it is salvation history: and it has selected and arranged and described events in order to bring out this point of view . . . that God has acted to save men.

Leonard Johnston

The Bible . . . is the classical book of noble ethical sentiment. In it the mortal fear, the overflowing hope, the quivering longings of the human soul . . . have found their first, their freshest, their fittest utterance.

A. Adler

Thanks to God whose Word is published
in the tongues of every race
See its glory undiminished
by the change of time or place
God has spoken:
Praise him for his open Word.

R. T. Brooks

I have read the most important so-called biographies of Jesus; in none of them do I find so much religious life as in the Gospels. The Gospels have the very smell of reality.

Thomas G. Masaryk

The crucial truths revealed in the Bible are not timeless truths about God and man; they are rather historical truths, truths regarding events which took place in time but which were invested by God with eternal significance.

John A. Mackay

The Old Testament challenges us to see this drama (of history) as God's drama and to play our role in the light of the continuing pressure of the purposes of God in all events, the God who has made himself known in that part of the drama which is the history of the Hebrews.

Robert Davidson

The New Testament is the history of the life and the testimony of common men who rallied to the fellowship of Jesus Christ and who by their faith and preaching remade a world that was under the thrall of a Roman army.

Woodrow Wilson

These sacred words give you the very image of Christ speaking, healing, dying, rising again, and make him so present, that were he before your very eyes you would not more truly see him.

Desiderius Erasmus

The supreme fact about the Bible is that it is substantially a history of the growth of the idea of God.

St. John Ervine

The immortal epic of a people's confused, faltering, but indomitable struggle after a nobler life in a happier world.

Lewis Browne

P

PARABLES

Parables

If we Christians wish to understand the psalms, we must bear in mind that the roots of their thought lie in the past, in the Old Testament, while their blossoming reaches out into the far future, to the end of the world, to heaven itself.

P. Druvers

Unspeakable mysteries in the Scriptures are often delivered in a vulgar and illustrative way; and being written unto man, are delivered, not as they truly are, but as they may be understood.

Thomas Browne

Because it was the message of God to humanity, the Gospel could only reveal itself in the simplest of garments.

Adolf Deissmann

Every idea in the Bible started from primitive and childlike origins and, with however many setbacks and delays, grew in scope and height toward the culmination in Christ's Gospel.

Harry Emerson Fosdick

The Bible is a window in this prison-world through which we may look into eternity.

Timothy Dwight

There were long ago men more ancient than any of the philosophers now in repute, men who were happy, upright, and beloved of God, who spoke by the divine Spirit and gave oracles of the future which are now coming to pass. These men are called prophets.

St. Justin Martyr

The modern conception of history has its roots in the Biblical story of Jahveh and of the world which He creates as the scene for the unfolding of a divine plan.

Morris R. Cohen

The men of God were spirit-borne and became prophets; being breathed upon by God Himself and made wise, they were taught of God, holy and just.

Theophilus of Antioch

The prophets . . . are the beating hearts of the Old Testament.

Walter Rauschenbusch

The early Hebrews had created the Bible out of their lives; their descendants created their lives out of the Bible.

Abraham Leon Sachar

The Bible teaches that demons are real, and are capable of entering and controlling people. They are spoken of as unclean, violent and malicious. All outside of Christ are in danger of demon possession.

Billy Graham

Men sometimes affect to deny the depravity of our race; but it is as clearly taught in the lawyer's office and in courts of justice as in the Bible itself.

Tryon Edwards

Demon possession is presented in Scripture as a dreadful reality. The supposition that the demoniacs of the Gospels were only mentally ill is fallacious.

Harold Lindsell

Foul shame and scorn be on ye all
Who turn the good to evil,
And steal the Bible from the Lord,
To give it to the Devil!

John Greenleaf Whittier

Fear is the denomination of the Old Testament; belief is the denomination of the New.

Benjamin Whichcote

In the Law is the shadow, in the Gospel is the Truth . . . in the former we are slaves, in the latter the Lord Who is present speaks; in the former are promises, in the latter the fulfillment; in the former are the beginnings, in the latter their completion.

St. Jerome

The Bible leads us to Jesus, the inexhaustible, the ever unfolding revelation of God.

George Macdonald

Christ is the master; the Scriptures are only the servant.

Martin Luther

Here you will find the cradle and swaddling clothes in which Christ lies, to which the angel directs the shepherds. They are poor and mean swaddling clothes, but precious is the treasure, Christ, who lies in them.

Martin Luther

One mighty representative of the whole spiritual life of humanity.

Helen Keller

Allegoristic exegesis is almost purely subjective. He who uses it can find in the Holy Book anything he has already in mind.

J. Lawson

Since God is known by what He has done, the Bible exists as a confessional recital of His acts, together with the teaching accompanying those acts, or inferred from them in the light of specific situations which the faithful confronted.

G. E. Wright

Man in the Bible is always on tiptoe, straining his eyes for the first light of dawn.

George A. Buttrick

A parable of man's advance to the family, to the tribe, to a nation with a national ideal, to a nation with a universal ideal.

Franz Rosenzweig

RELEVANCE

Relevance

A plain old book, modest as nature itself . . . a book of an unpretending work-day appearance, like the sun that warms or the bread that nourishes us.

Heinrich Heine

No one, I venture, reading the Gospels attentively, but must feel, "If God ever spoke to man, this is what He would say."

John A. Cass

When you read God's word, you must constantly be saying to yourself, it is talking to me, and about me.

Søren Kierkegaard

You can learn more about human nature by reading the Bible than by living in New York.

William Lyon Phelps

There is nothing musty about the Gospel, and nothing misty about it either.

Oscar C. J. Hoffmann

The Christian feels that the tooth of time gnaws all books but the Bible. It has a pertinent relevance to every age. It has worked miracles by itself alone. It has made its way where no missionary had gone and has done the missionary's work. . . . Nineteen centuries of experience have tested the Book. It has passed through critical fires no other volume has suffered, and its spiritual truth has endured the flames and come out without so much as the smell of burning.

W. E. Sangster

The Bible experienced is God experienced in all the length and breadth and height and depth of His revelation and communication to man.

E. I. Watkin

It is just because the prophets and apostles are so in-dwelt by the Spirit of God that they are so robustly, freely, independently and concretely human. The incoming of God's Spirit does not eliminate their human qualities so that they become mere puppets of God, but in the fullest sense it makes them men of God.

J. D. Smart

There is not a verse (of the Bible), not a word, but is thick-studded with human emotion.

Walt Whitman

Those who do not want the sexual aspect of life included in the portrayal of real-life situations had better burn their Bibles as well as abstain from the movies.

James A. Pike

Sacred history is not restricted to the contents of the Bible, but is still going on; we are living in sacred history.

Jean Danielou

Old Testament religion is clearly about this world, and about nothing else.

John Mac Murray

The ancient prophets walk through the world of Judaism, like living geniuses reawaking from generation to generation.

Leo Baeck

They (Old Testament Prophets) offered to the unfortunate of the earth a vision of brotherhood that became the precious and unforgotten heritage of many generations.

Will Durant

Whenever we hear the Word of God in the human word, the message of the Bible becomes no longer a message out of the past, but an event in the present.

Alan Richardson and W. Schweitzer

77

You can only find God in the now. Our God is a God that moves. Only in the contemporaneous does God converse with men. His very name is "Now," "I am that I am," and, "I will be that I will be." God is still sovereign. He is at the hub, while the church gnaws its fingers in mystification that the vast majority in East and West pass us by as irrelevant. All through the Bible the contemporary situation is the arena in which you meet God.

George F. MacLeod

In the Bible God's name is named, not as philosophers do it, as the name of a timeless Being, surpassing the world, alien and supreme, but as the name of the living, acting, working Subject who makes Himself known.

Karl Barth

I have sometimes seen more in a line of the Bible than I could well tell how to stand under, and yet another time the whole Bible hath been to me as dry as a stick.

John Bunyan

The scriptural renascence is largely an effort to enable the Christian to hear the Word of God in the twentieth century as it was heard in the first—as salvation history, as the good news of God.

Philip Scharper

The whole Bible, from cover to cover, is concerned with this riddle . . . whether or not the universe at its center is or ever was intelligent and purposeful and kind; if it means something still, and means that something intensely; if, as someone has put it, there is a great yawning hole in the middle of things, through which all energy and vision, all lives and prayers and sacrifice, shall be poured at the last and lost—or if God is there! These (sixty-six) books gather all their things together, fill their lungs, and with a mighty shout proclaim that he is!

Paul E. Scherer

We have seen Scripture become mere plain philosophy, the words of Christ the words of a teacher who has seen the ultimate realities and speaks them very simply, with the simplicity of utter authority.

Woodrow Wilson

Talk about the questions of the day; there is but one question, and that is the Gospel. It can and will correct everything needing correction.

William E. Gladstone

The Bible was never intended to be a book for scholars and specialists only. From the very beginning it was intended to be everybody's book, and that is what it continues to be.

F. F. Bruce

We do not have a personal Gospel and a social gospel. There is one Gospel, and one Gospel only, and that Gospel is the Gospel of God—this indivisible message from God has its individual application and its social application. It has the power to redeem the individual and also the power to redeem social order.

Jesse M. Bader

It is, as it were, a kind of river, if I may so liken it, which is both shallow and deep, wherein both the lamb may find a footing and the elephant float at large.

St. Gregory The Great

The Gospel is a social message, solemn and over-powering in its force; it is the proclamation of solidarity and brotherliness, in favor of the poor.

Adolf von Harnack

So far as such equality, liberty and fraternity are included under the democratic principles which assume the same names, the Bible is the most democratic book in the world.

Thomas H. Huxley

Throughout the history of the Western World the Scriptures have been the great instigators of revolt against the worst forms of clerical and political despotism. The Bible has been the Magna Charta of the poor and of the oppressed.

Thomas H. Huxley

The gospel belongs to the poor and sorrowful, and not to princes and courtiers who live in continual joy and delight, in security, void of all tribulation.

Martin Luther

The Bible is for the government of the people, by the people, and for the people.

John Wycliffe

The spirit of the gospel is democratic. The tendency of the Gospel is leveling; leveling up, not down. It is carrying the poor and the multitude onward and upward.

Henry Ward Beecher

The Bible is the only literature in the world up to our century which looks at women as human beings, no better and no worse than men.

Edith Hamilton

The Bible is the sheet anchor of our liberties. Write its principles upon your heart and practice them in your lives.

Ulysses S. Grant

The whole Bible is a hymn to Justice,—that is, in the Hebrew style, to charity, to kindness to the weak on the part of the strong, to voluntary renunciation of the privilege of power.

P. J. Proundhon

Strange, after having passed the whole of my life in gliding about the dancing floors of philosophy, and abandoning myself to all the orgies of the intellect, and dallying with systems without ever being satisfied—I have suddenly arrived at the same point of view as Uncle Tom, taking my stand on the Bible and kneeling beside my black brother in prayer in the same act of devotion.

Heinrich Heine

It is impossible mentally or socially to enslave a Bible-reading people.

Horace Greeley

The central ideas of Scripture, in whatever changing categories they may be phrased, seem to me the hope of man's individual and social life.

Harry Emerson Fosdick

Suppose a nation in some distant region should take the Bible for their only lawbook, and every member should regulate his conduct by the precepts there exhibited! . . . What a Utopia; what a Paradise would this region be!

John Quincy Adams

S

STUDY

Study

There is no universal precept, either divine or apostolic, that all the faithful—every man, woman and child—should personally read the Bible; Heaven is open to illiterates. It is the doctrine of the Bible that matters, not knowledge of the letter.

W. Leonard and B. Orchard

Blessed Lord, who has caused all holy Scriptures to be written for our learning; Grant that we may . . . hear them, read, mark, learn and inwardly digest them.

Book of Common Prayer

Everything in the Sacred Books shines and glistens, even in its outer shell: but the marrow of it is sweeter: if you want the kernel, you must break the shell.

St. Jerome

Scripture is the school of the Holy Spirit, in which, as nothing is omitted that is both necessary and useful to know, so nothing is taught but what is expedient to know.

John Calvin

The best way to get to know the Bible is to my mind to read it as a child aloud, in common, either at home or in school.

Nicolette Gray

One chapter a day was all we took. We searched that carefully, and noted down with miser eagerness everything which seemed to us to have an important bearing upon any point in our scheme . . . but by dint of this practice we ourselves grew daily in the power of judging; and not only that, but the skill and the power of seeing, too; till by the time we were half through the Bible, we were just fit to begin again at the beginning. And so we did. . . .

Susan Warner

By the study of what other book could children be so much humanized and made to feel that each figure in the vast historical procession fills, like themselves but a momentary space in the interval between eternities.

Thomas H. Huxley

Our one desire for all the Church's children is that, being saturated with the Bible, they may arrive at the all-surpassing knowledge of Jesus Christ.

Pope Benedict XV

Christian men and women, old and young, should study fast in the New Testament, for it is of full authority, and open to understanding of simple men, as to the points that be most needful to salvation.

John Wycliffe

Ignorance of the Bible means ignorance of Christ.

St. Jerome

I thoroughly believe in a university education for both men and women; but I believe a knowledge of the Bible without a college course is more valuable than a college course without the Bible.

William Lyon Phelps

A thorough knowledge of the Bible is worth more than a college education.

Theodore Roosevelt

I consider an intimate knowledge of the Bible an indispensable qualification of a well-educated man.

Robert A. Millikan

If a man's Bible is coming apart, it is an indication that he himself is fairly well put together.

James E. Jennings

Apply yourself to the whole text, and apply the whole text to yourself.

Johannes Albrecht Bengel

A man speaks more or less wisely in proportion as he has made more or less progress in Holy Scriptures.

St. Augustine of Hippo

Each place of holy writ, both open and dark, teaches meekness and charity; and therefore he that keepeth meekness and charity hath the true understanding and perfection of all holy writ. . . . Therefore no simple man of wit be afraid unmeasurable to study in the text of holy writ.

John Wycliffe

The Bible becomes even more beautiful the more it is understood.

Johann W. von Goethe

The more deeply we enter into the study the more effect the teachings of Holy Writ will have over our minds.

Aidan Gasquet

As in Paradise, God walks in the Holy Scriptures, seeking man. When a sinner reads these Scriptures, he hears God's voice saying, "Adam, where art thou?"

St. Ambrose

The study of inspired Scripture is the chief way of finding our duty.

St. Basil

I have always had a Bible in my parlor these many years, and ofttimes when the weather hath been foul, and that I have had no other book to read on, and have wanted company to play at cards or at tables with me, I have read in those books.

John Harrington

Often read the divine Scriptures; yea, let holy reading be always in thy hand; study that which thou thyself must preach.

St. Jerome

The best preachers of all ages . . . have gratefully acknowledged that they owed their repute chiefly to the assiduous use of the Bible, and to devout meditation on its pages.

Pope Leo XIII

I have made it a practice for several years to read the Bible through in the course of every year. I usually devote to this reading the first hour after I rise in the morning.

John Quincy Adams

The study of God's Word, for the purpose of discovering God's will, is the secret discipline which has formed the greatest characters.

James W. Alexander

When we consider the Old Testament as written by divine inspiration, and preserved, beyond the time of its own Dispensation, for us Christians . . . we ought not surely to read any portion of it with indifference, nay without great and anxious interest. . . . Christ and His Apostles cannot have put the Law and the Prophets into our hands for nothing.

John Henry Newman

The Bible forms the theme of Christian medication, Christian preaching, and Christian art: it is also the staple of the liturgy of the Church. It is a book to be meditated, and not gabbled over.

Joseph Rickaby

A man who is well grounded in the testimonies of the Scriptures is the bulwark of the Church.

St. Jerome

One must read the Bible continually to prevent the image of truth being obscured in us.

Julian Green

If all who believe in Christ will read the Scriptures in prayerful meditation and incorporate its teaching into their lives, they will not only be drawn closer to Christ, but to one another.

Augustin Bea

And none can fail to see what profit and sweet tranquility must result in well-disposed souls from such devout reading of the Bible. Whoever comes to it in pity, faith and humility, and with a determination to make progress in it, will assuredly find therein and will eat the "bread that comes down from heaven."

Pope Benedict XV

Prayer, in its turn, needs to be sustained by reading Holy Scripture.

François Fénelon

The liturgical worshipper prays the Bible, directly when he prays in the words of Scripture, indirectly when he reads or hears the lesson in the same attitude of prayer. . . . He who thus prays the Bible with the liturgy penetrates the letter of Scripture to its inner spirit.

E. I. Watkin

Holy Bible, book divine,
Precious treasure, thou art mine;
Mine to teach me whence I came,
Mine to teach me what I am.

John Burton

When one rereads the Bible as a Jew, Protestant, Orthodox or Roman Catholic, he may read it as a mirror of his preconceptions; when encouraged to read it in the contexts of other traditions, he is apt to find something hitherto overlooked.

Martin E. Marty

I discover an arrant laziness in my soul. For when I am to read a chapter in the Bible, before I begin I look where it endeth. And if it endeth not on the same side, I cannot keep my hands from turning over the leaf, to measure the length thereof on the other side; if it swells to many verses, I begin to grudge. Surely my heart is not rightly affected. Were I truly hungry after heavenly food, I would not complain of meat. Scourge, Lord, this laziness of my soul; make the reading of thy Word not a penance but a pleasure unto me; so I may esteem that chapter in Thy Word the best which is the longest.

Thomas Fuller

If thou wilt profit by reading of Scripture read meekly, simply, and faithfully, and never desire to have thereby the name of cunning.

Thomas à Kempis

If a man is not familiar with the Bible, he has suffered a loss which he had better make all possible haste to correct.

Theodore Roosevelt

If God is reality, and the soul is a reality, and you are an immortal being, what are you doing with your Bible shut?

Herrick Johnson

There is no attack of the enemy so violent, that is, no temptation so formidable, that an eager study of the Scriptures will not easily beat off.

Desiderius Erasmus

Man has deprived himself of the best there is in the world who has deprived himself of this: a knowledge of the Bible. . . . This book is the one supreme source of revelation, the revelation of the meaning of life, the nature of God, and the spiritual nature and need of men. It is a book which reveals every man to himself as a distinct moral agent, responsible not to men, not even to those men whom he has put over him in authority, but responsible through his own conscience to his Lord and Maker. Whenever a man sees this vision, he stands up a free man whatever may be the circumstances of his life.

Woodrow Wilson

Lay hold on the Bible until the Bible lays hold on you.

Will H. Houghton

WORD OF GOD

Word of God

We believe and confess that the Canonical Scriptures of the Old and New Testaments are the true Word of God, and have sufficient authority in and of themselves, and not from men. . . . They contain all that is necessary to a saving faith and a holy life; and hence nothing could be added to or taken from them.

Henry Bullinger

Inspiration . . . is the determining influence exercised by the Holy Spirit on the writers of the Old and New Testaments in order that they might proclaim and set down in an exact and authentic way the message as received from God.

René Pache

The Scripture, collecting in our minds the otherwise confused notions of Deity, dispels the darkness and gives us a clear view of the true God.

John Calvin

Nothing is of faith that is not in Scripture.

Benjamin Whichcote

All teaching and all truth and all doctrine must be tested in the light of the Scriptures.

D. Martin Lloyd-Jones

It makes no difference at all that the Holy Ghost should have taken men to be as it were his tools in writing, as it forsooth the man who were inspired, but not the divine author, might let fall some error. Not so, for he himself so stirred and roused them by his supernatural power and wrote, and was so present to them in their writing that they conceived correctly, and were minded to write faithfully, and expressed fittingly with unfailing truth, all those things and those only which he bade them write.

Pope Benedict XV

═══════

The Gospel as the Word of God is properly spoken to the ear and not written for the eye.

Amos N. Wilder

═══════

The Scriptures read are the same thing to us which the same doctrine was when it was preached by the disciples of our Blessed Lord; and we are to learn of either with the same dispositions.

Jerome Taylor

═══════

It is only in the Scriptures that the Lord hath been pleased to preserve his truth in perpetual remembrance; it obtains the same complete credit and authority with believers, where they are satisfied of its divine origin, as if they heard the very words pronounced by God Himself.

John Calvin

He then Himself wrote them. Who dictated the thing that should be written. He did Himself write them Who both was present as the Inspirer in the Saint's work, and by the mouth of the writer has consigned to us His acts as patterns for our imitation.

St. Gregory The Great

God preaches to us in the Scripture, and by his secret assistances and by spiritual thoughts and holy motions.

Jeremy Taylor

Since they wrote the things which He showed and uttered to them, it cannot be pretended that He is not the writer; for His members executed what their head dictated.

St. Augustine of Hippo

The writer said just what God would have him say, and said it because God moved him to do so.

R. Clarke

The office of a commentator is to set forth not what he himself would prefer but what his author says.

St. Jerome

The word of God is all those commandments and revelations, those promises and threatenings, the stories and sermons recorded in the Bible; nothing else is the word of God.

Jeremy Taylor

Since the Bible as salvation history is primarily God's self-revelation, God must be regarded as principal Author of Scripture. At the same time, and of necessity, the Bible, written by men, is an epiphany of those men's response of loving obedience and faith to God's message.

David M. Stanley

The difference between the Old and the New Testaments is the difference between a man who said "There is nothing new under the sun" and a God who says "Behold, I make all things new."

Ronald A. Knox

The authority of the New Testament is absolute in so far as it brings us the Word of God and His grace. This message is found by the guidance of the spirit and normally within the followship of the Church.

R. Newton Flew

It is the holiness of our Lord's heart that fills the New Testament full and makes it the unparalleled and unapproachable Book that it is.

Alexander Whyte

This is the fundamental view of the Bible—man gains his distinctiveness, his truly human nature, by the fact that God speaks to him and that man in faith receives this Word and answers it with the "yes" of faith.

Emil Brunner

Peruse the words of our philosophers with all their pomp of diction; how mean, how contemptible they are, compared with the Scriptures. Is it possible that a book at once so simple and so sublime should be merely the work of man?

Jean Jacques Rousseau

My heart has always assured me that the gospel of Jesus Christ must be Divine Reality.

Daniel Webster

In the Old Testament of the Jews, the book of Divine righteousness, there are men, events and words so great that there is nothing in Greek or Indian literature to compare with it.

Friedrich Nietzsche

This is the people's book of revelation, revelation of themselves not alone, but revelation of life and of peace.

Woodrow Wilson

We are compelled to concede to the Papists that they have the Word of God, that we received it from them; and that without them we should have no knowledge of it at all.

Martin Luther

The recognition of the authority of the Bible was not an innovation; theoretically it had been supreme since an early day.

A. C. McGiffert

———

The Bible is God's revelation to man, his guide, his light.

Alfred Armand Montapert

———

It nowhere lays claim to be regarded as the Word, the Way, the Truth. The Bible leads us to Jesus, the inexhaustible, the even unfolding Revelation of God.

George Macdonald

———

The Word of God is in the Bible as the soul is in the body.

Peter T. Forsyth

———

The Word of God is not based on and contained in Christian faith, but Christian faith is based on and contained in the Word of God.

Karl Barth

———

No matter what the human intermediaries may be, it is the living and personal Word of God which presents the truths of faith to the soul until the end of time.

Jean Mouroux

The authority of the Bible reposes in the fact that, in statements some right and some wrong, and in practical application some of which is disputable and some even more dubious, a unified witness is borne to Him who is at the centre of the Gospel.

J. K. S. Reid

The truly wise man is he who believes the Bible against the opinions of any man. If the Bible says one thing, and any body of men says another, the wise man will decide, "This book is the Word of him who cannot lie."

R. A. Torrey

I wish to show that there is one wisdom which is perfect, and that this is contained in the Scriptures.

Roger Bacon

The Bible is God's book because it is in a unique and universal sense Man's book. It is the record of and the vehicle for transmitting a great human experience, an experience of God, of human need, and of God's response to that need.

Richard Brook

The Gospel is eternal: from age to age we may catch new accents in God's Word to men, but the Word itself is from the foundation of the world.

Interpreter's Bible

PART II

WHAT THE BIBLE SAYS

ACCEPTANCE
ASKING FOR HELP

Acceptance

I have learned, in whatsoever state I am, therewith to be content. I know both how to be abased, and I know how to abound: everywhere and in all things I am instructed both to be full and to be hungry, both to abound and to suffer need. I can do all things through Christ which strengtheneth me.

Philippians 4:11−13

Let your conversation be without covetousness; and be content with such things as ye have: for he hath said, I will never leave thee, nor forsake thee.

Hebrews 13:5

Take therefore no thought for the morrow: for the morrow shall take thought for the things of itself. Sufficient unto the day is the evil thereof.

Matthew 6:34

Know ye not that ye are the temple of God, and that the Spirit of God dwelleth in you?

1 Corinthians 3:16

Unto the pure all things are pure.

Titus 1:15

O Lord, thou hast searched me, and known me.
Thou knowest my downsitting and mine uprising;
thou understandest my thought afar off.
Thou compassest my path and my lying down,
and art acquainted with all my ways.
For there is not a word in my tongue,
but, lo, O Lord, thou knowest it altogether.
Thou hast beset me behind and before,
and laid thine hand upon me.
Such knowledge is too wonderful for me;
it is high, I cannot attain unto it.

Whither shall I go from thy Spirit?
Or whither shall I flee from thy presence?
If I ascend up into heaven, thou art there:
if I make my bed in hell, behold, thou art there.
If I take the wings of the morning,
    and dwell in the uttermost parts of the sea;
even there shall thy hand lead me,
and thy right hand shall hold me.
If I say, Surely the darkness shall cover me;
even the night shall be light about me.
Yea, the darkness hideth not from thee;
but the night shineth as the day:
the darkness and the light are both
    alike to thee.

Search me, O God, and know my heart:
try me, and know my thoughts:
and see if there be any wicked way in me,
and lead me in the way everlasting.

Psalm 139:1–12, 23, 24

I have seen the travail, which God hath given to the sons of men to be exercised in it. He hath made every thing beautiful in his time: also he hath set the world in their heart, so that no man can find out the work that God maketh from the beginning to the end.

Ecclesiastes 3:10, 11

Draw nigh to God and he will draw nigh to you.

James 4:8

Behold, I stand at the door, and knock: if any man hear my voice, and open the door, I will come in to him, and will sup with him, and he with me.

Revelation 3:20

I am the door: by me if any man enter in, he shall be saved, and shall go in and out, and find pasture.

John 10:9

The Lord gave, and the Lord hath taken away; blessed be the name of the Lord.

Job 1:21

Man dieth, and wasteth away: yea, man giveth up the ghost, and where is he?

Job 14:10

To every thing there is a season, and a time to every purpose under the heaven: a time to be born, and a time to die; a time to plant, and a time to pluck up that which is planted; a time to kill, and a time to heal; a time to break down, and a time to build up; a time to weep, and a time to laugh; a time to mourn, and a time to dance; a time to cast away stones, and a time to gather stones together; a time to embrace, and a time to refrain from embracing; a time to get, and a time to lose; a time to keep, and a time to cast away; a time to rend, and a time to sew; a time to keep silence, and a time to speak; a time to love, and a time to hate; a time of war, and a time of peace.

Ecclesiastes 3:1−8

The hour is coming, in the which all that are in the graves shall hear his voice, and shall come forth.

John 5:28, 29

Weep ye not for the dead, neither bemoan him.

Jeremiah 22:10

For dust thou art, and unto dust shalt thou return.

Genesis 3:19

We all do fade as a leaf.

Isaiah 64:6

Thou shalt come to thy grave in a full age, like as a shock of corn cometh in in his season.

Job 5:26

Asking for Help

Cast thy burden upon the Lord,
and he shall sustain thee:
he shall never suffer the righteous to
   be moved.

Psalm 55:22

===

I sought the Lord, and he heard me.

Psalm 34:4

===

Like as a father pitieth his children,
so the Lord pitieth them that fear him.
For he knoweth our frame;
he remembereth that we are dust.

Psalm 103:13, 14

===

The righteous cry, and the Lord heareth,
and delivereth them out of all their troubles.

Psalm 34:17

How amiable are thy tabernacles,
   O Lord of hosts!
My soul longeth, yea, even fainteth for
   the courts of the Lord:
my heart and my flesh crieth out
   for the living God.

Blessed are they that dwell in thy house:
they will be still praising thee.

O Lord of hosts, blessed is the man that
   trusteth in thee.

Psalm 84:1, 2, 4, 12

They that wait upon the Lord shall renew their strength.

Isaiah 40:31

Then shalt thou call, and the Lord shall answer; thou shalt
cry, and he shall say, Here I am.

Isaiah 58:9

My God, my God, why hast thou
   forsaken me?
Why art thou so far from helping me,
   and from the words of my roaring?

Psalm 22:1

For thou art my hope, O Lord God:
thou art my trust from my youth.
By thee have I been holden up from the womb:
thou art he that took me out of my mother's bowels:
my praise shall be continually of thee.

I am as a wonder unto many;
but thou art my strong refuge.

Cast me not off in the time of old age;
forsake me not when my strength faileth.

O God, thou hast taught me from my youth:
and hitherto have I declared thy wondrous works.
Now also when I am old and grayheaded,
O God, forsake me not;
until I have showed thy strength unto this generation,
and thy power to every one that is to come.

Psalm 71:5—7, 9, 17, 18

My voice shalt thou hear in the morning,
  O Lord;
in the morning will I direct my prayer
  unto thee,
and will look up.

Psalm 5:3

We know not what we should pray for as we ought: but the Spirit itself maketh intercession for us with groanings which cannot be uttered.

Romans 8:26

Save me, O God;
for the waters are come in unto
   my soul.
I sink in deep mire,
where there is no standing:
I am come into deep waters,
where the floods overflow me.

Psalm 69:1, 2

I cried unto the Lord with my voice;
with my voice unto the Lord did I make my supplication.
I poured out my complaint before him;
I showed before him my trouble.
When my spirit was overwhelmed within me,
then thou knewest my path.

Psalm 142:1−3

Thou art he that took me out of the womb:
thou didst make me hope when I was
   upon my mother's breasts.
I was cast upon thee from the womb:
thou art my God from my mother's belly.
Be not far from me; for trouble is near;
for there is none to help.

Psalm 22:9−11

I will lift up mine eyes unto the hills,
from whence cometh my help.
My help cometh from the Lord,
which made heaven and earth.

Psalm 121:1, 2

Create in me a clean heart, O God;
and renew a right spirit within me.
Cast me not away from thy presence;
and take not thy Holy Spirit from me.
Restore unto me the joy of thy salvation;
and uphold me with thy free Spirit.

Psalm 51:10–12

Blessed be God,
which hath not turned away my prayer,
nor his mercy from me.

Psalm 66:20

The effectual fervent prayer of a righteous man availeth
much.

James 5:16

Be careful for nothing; but in every thing by prayer and
supplication with thanksgiving let your requests be made
known unto God.

Philippians 4:6

When ye pray, use not vain repetitions.

Matthew 6:7

117

Lead me in thy truth, and teach me:
for thou art the God of my salvation;
on thee do I wait all the day.

Remember, O Lord, thy tender mercies and
   thy loving-kindness;
for they have been ever of old.
Remember not the sins of my youth.

Psalm 25:5−7

If any of you lack wisdom, let him ask of God, that giveth to all men liberally, and upbraideth not; and it shall be given him. But let him ask in faith, nothing wavering: for he that wavereth is like a wave of the sea driven with the wind and tossed.

James 1:5, 6

This is the confidence that we have in him, that, if we ask any thing according to his will, he heareth us: and if we know that he hear us, whatsoever we ask, we know that we have the petitions that we desired of him.

1 John 5:14, 15

Your Father knoweth what things ye have need of, before ye ask him.

Matthew 6:8

After this manner therefore pray ye:
  Our Father which art in heaven,
Hallowed by thy name.
  Thy kingdom come.
Thy will be done
  in earth, as it is in heaven.
Give us this day our daily bread.
  And forgive us our debts,
as we forgive our debtors.
  And lead us not into temptation,
but deliver us from evil:
  For thine is the kingdom, and the power,
and the glory, for ever.
  Amen.

Matthew 6:9—13

Whatsoever ye shall ask in my name, that will I do, that the Father may be glorified in the Son. If ye shall ask any thing in my name, I will do it.

John 14:13, 14

Ask, and it shall be given you; seek, and ye shall find; knock, and it shall be opened unto you: for every one that asketh receiveth; and he that seeketh findeth; and to him that knocketh it shall be opened.

Matthew 7:7, 8

C

CHARITY
COMFORT
COMMANDMENTS

Charity

Give, and it shall be given unto you; good measure, pressed down, and shaken together, and running over, shall men give into your bosom. For with the same measure that ye mete withal it shall be measured to you again.

Luke 6:38

Put on charity, which is the bond of perfectness.

Colossians 3:14

Now abideth faith, hope, charity, these three; but the greatest of these is charity.

1 Corinthians 13:13

From him that would borrow of thee turn not thou away.

Matthew 5:42

Whosoever shall give to drink unto one of these little ones a cup of cold water only in the name of a disciple, verily I say unto you, he shall in no wise lose his reward.

Matthew 10:42

He that hath two coats, let him impart to him that hath none; and he that hath meat, let him do likewise.

Luke 3:11

The end of all things is at hand: be ye therefore sober, and watch unto prayer. And above all things have fervent charity among yourselves: for charity shall cover the multitude of sins. Use hospitality one to another without grudging.

1 Peter 4:7–9

Be not forgetful to entertain strangers: for therefore some have entertained angels unawares.

Hebrews 13:2

When thou makest a dinner or a supper, call not thy friends, nor thy brethren, neither thy kinsmen, nor thy rich neighbors; lest they also bid thee again, and a recompense be made thee. But when thou makest a feast, call the poor, the maimed, the lame, the blind: and thou shalt be blessed; for they cannot recompense thee: for thou shalt be recompensed at the resurrection of the just.

Luke 14:12–14

Fear not, little flock; for it is your Father's good pleasure to give you the kingdom. Sell that ye have, and give alms; provide yourselves bags which wax not old, a treasure in the heavens that faileth not, where no thief approacheth, neither moth corrupteth. For where your treasure is, there will your heart be also.

Luke 12:32–34

He spake a parable unto them, saying, The ground of a certain rich man brought forth plentifully: and he thought within himself, saying, What shall I do, because I have no room where to bestow my fruits? And he said, This will I do: I will pull down my barns, and build greater; and there will I bestow all my fruits and my goods. And I will say to my soul, Soul, thou hast much goods laid up for many years; take thine ease, eat, drink, and be merry. But God said unto him, Thou fool, this night thy soul shall be required of thee: then whose shall those things be, which thou hast provided? So is he that layeth up treasure for himself, and is not rich toward God.

Luke 12:16−21

―――

Whoso hath this world's good, and seeth his brother have need, and shutteth up his bowels of compassion from him, how dwelleth the love of God in him? My little children, let us not love in word, neither in tongue; but in deed and in truth.

1 John 3:17, 18

―――

Consider the ravens: for they neither sow nor reap; which neither have storeroom nor barn; and God feedeth them: how much more are ye better than the fowls?

Luke 12:24

―――

Unto whomsoever much is given, of him shall be much required; and to whom men have committed much, of him they will ask the more.

Luke 12:48

Jesus said unto him, If thou wilt be perfect, go and sell that thou hast, and give to the poor, and thou shalt have treasure in heaven: and come and follow me. But when the young man heard that saying, he went away sorrowful: for he had great possessions. Then said Jesus unto his disciples, Verily I say unto you, That a rich man shall hardly enter into the kingdom of heaven. And again I say unto you, It is easier for a camel to go through the eye of a needle, than for a rich man to enter into the kingdom of God. When his disciples heard it, they were exceedingly amazed, saying, Who then can be saved?

Matthew 19:21−25

If thou draw out thy soul to the hungry, and satisfy the afflicted soul; then shall thy light rise in obscurity, and thy darkness be as the noonday.

Isaiah 58:10

He that hath pity upon the poor lendeth unto the Lord; and that which he hath given will he pay him again.

Proverbs 19:17

He that giveth unto the poor shall not lack.

Proverbs 28:27

Blessed is he that considereth the poor.

Psalm 41:1

Comfort

The Lord is nigh unto them that are
   of a broken heart;
and saveth such as be of a contrite spirit.

Psalm 34:18

But I am poor and needy;
yet the Lord thinketh upon me.

Psalm 40:17

He healeth the broken in heart,
and bindeth up their wounds.

Psalm 147:3

The Lord hath comforted his people, and will have mercy
upon his afflicted.

Isaiah 49:13

If any man thirst, let him come unto me, and drink.

John 7:37

To this man will I look [saith the Lord,] even to him that is
poor and of a contrite spirit, and trembleth at my word.

Isaiah 66:2

Blessed be God, even the Father of our Lord Jesus Christ, the Father of mercies, and the God of all comfort; who comforteth us in all our tribulation, that we may be able to comfort them which are in any trouble, by the comfort wherewith we ourselves are comforted of God.

2 Corinthians 1:3, 4

For the mountains shall depart, and the hills be removed; but my kindness shall not depart from thee, neither shall the covenant of my peace be removed, saith the Lord that hath mercy on thee.

Isaiah 54:10

The blessing of the Lord, it maketh rich, and he addeth no sorrow with it.

Proverbs 10:22

Let your speech be always with grace, seasoned with salt, that ye may know how ye ought to answer every man.

Colossians 4:6

But I am like a green olive tree in the
    house of God:
I trust in the mercy of God for ever and
    ever.

Psalm 52:8

Blessed are the poor in spirit: for theirs is the kingdom of heaven. Blessed are they that mourn: for they shall be comforted. Blessed are the meek: for they shall inherit the earth. Blessed are they which do hunger and thirst after righteousness: for they shall be filled. Blessed are the merciful: for they shall obtain mercy. Blessed are the pure in heart: for they shall see God. Blessed are the peacemakers: for they shall be called children of God.

Matthew 5:3−9

Lo, children are a heritage of the Lord:
and the fruit of the womb is his reward.
As arrows are in the hand of a mighty man;
so are children of the youth.

Psalm 127:3, 4

The Lord bless thee, and keep thee: the Lord make his face shine upon thee, and be gracious unto thee: the Lord lift up his countenance upon thee, and give thee peace.

Numbers 6:24−26

Great peace have they which love thy law:
and nothing shall offend them.

Psalm 119:165

The peace of God, which passeth all understanding, shall keep your hearts and minds through Christ Jesus.

Philippians 4:7

Peace I leave with you, my peace I give unto you: not as the world giveth, give I unto you. Let not your heart be troubled, neither let it be afraid.

John 14:27

Those things I have spoken unto you, that in me ye might have peace. In the world ye shall have tribulation: but be of good cheer; I have overcome the world.

John 16:33

I will not leave you comfortless: I will come to you.

John 14:18

Behold, we count them happy which endure. Ye have heard of the patience of Job, and have seen the end of the Lord; that the Lord is very pitiful, and of tender mercy.

James 5:11

Come unto me, all ye that labor and are heavy laden, and I will give you rest.

Matthew 11:28

The sabbath was made for man, and not man for the sabbath.

Mark 2:27

The Lord is my shepherd; I shall not want.
He maketh me to lie down in green pastures:
he leadeth me beside the still waters.
He restoreth my soul:
he leadeth me in the paths of righteousness
    for his name's sake.

Yea, though I walk through the valley of
    the shadow of death,
I will fear no evil: for thou art with me;
thy rod and thy staff they comfort me.

Thou preparest a table before me in the
    presence of mine enemies:
thou anointest my head with oil;
my cup runneth over.
Surely goodness and mercy shall follow me
    all the days of my life:
and I will dwell in the house of
    the Lord forever.

Psalm 23

They shall hunger no more, neither thirst any more; neither shall the sun light on them, nor any heat. For the Lamb which is in the midst of the throne shall feed them, and shall lead them unto living fountains of waters: and God shall wipe away all tears from their eyes.

Revelation 7:16, 17

I heard a great voice out of heaven saying, Behold, the tabernacle of God is with men, and he will dwell with them, and they shall be his people, and God himself shall be with them, and be their God. And God shall wipe away all tears from their eyes; and there shall be no more death, neither sorrow, nor crying, neither shall there be any more pain: for the former things are passed away.

Revelation 21:3, 4

Commandments

For this commandment which I command thee this day, it is not hidden from thee, neither is it far off. It is not in heaven, that thou shouldest say, Who shall go up for us to heaven, and bring it unto us, that we may hear it, and do it? Neither is it beyond the sea, that thou shouldest say, Who shall go over the sea for us, and bring it unto us, that we may hear it, and do it? But the word is very nigh unto thee, in thy mouth, and in thy heart, that thou mayest do it. See, I have set before thee this day life and good, and death and evil; in that I command thee this day to love the Lord thy God, . . . that thou mayest live and multiply.

Deuteronomy 30:11−16

Thou shalt love the Lord thy God with all thy heart, and with all thy soul, and with all thy mind.

Matthew 22:37

If any man hear my words, and believe not, I judge him not: for I came not to judge the world, but to save the world. He that rejecteth me, and receiveth not my words, hath one that judgeth him: the word that I have spoken, the same shall judge him in the last day. For I have not spoken of myself; but the Father which sent me, he gave me a commandment, what I should say, and what I should speak. And I know that his commandment is life everlasting: whatsoever I speak therefore, even as the Father said unto me, so I speak.

John 12:47−50

And thou shalt love the Lord thy God with all thine heart, and with all thy soul, and with all thy might.

Deuteronomy 6:5

We love him, because he first loved us. If a man say, I love God, and hateth his brother, he is a liar: for he that loveth not his brother whom he hath seen, how can he love God whom he hath not seen? And this commandment have we from him, That he who loveth God love his brother also.

1 John 4:19−21

Whosoever hateth his brother is a murderer.

1 John 3:15

Not as though I wrote a new commandment unto thee, but that which we had from the beginning, that we love one another. And this is love, that we walk after his commandments. This is the commandment, That, as ye have heard from the beginning, ye should walk in it.

2 John 5, 6

A new commandment I give unto you, That ye love one another; as I have loved you, that ye also love one another. By this shall all men know that ye are my disciples, if ye have love one to another.

John 13:34, 35

Honor thy father and thy mother: that thy days may be long upon the land which the Lord thy God giveth thee.

Exodus 20:12

Thou shalt love thy neighbor as thyself.

Galatians 5:14

Love your enemies, bless them that curse you, do good to them that hate you, and pray for them which despitefully use you.

Matthew 5:44

Thou shalt not bear false witness against thy neighbor.

Exodus 20:16

Owe no man any thing, but to love one another: for he that loveth another hath fulfilled the law. For this, Thou shalt not commit adultery, Thou shalt not kill, Thou shalt not steal, Thou shalt not bear false witness, Thou shalt not covet; and if there be any other commandment, it is briefly comprehended in this saying, namely, Thou shalt love thy neighbor as thyself. Love worketh no ill to his neighbor: therefore love is the fulfilling of the law.

Romans 13:8−10

Love not the world, neither the things that are in the world. If any man love the world, the love of the Father is not in him. For all that is in the world, the lust of the flesh, and the lust of the eyes, and the pride of life, is not of the Father, but is of the world. And the world passeth away, and the lust thereof: but he that doeth the will of God abideth for ever.

1 John 2:15−17

Render . . . unto Caesar the things which are Caesar's; and unto God the things that are God's.

Matthew 22:21

Keep thy heart with all diligence; for out of it are the issues of life. Put away from thee a froward mouth, and perverse lips put afar from thee. Let thine eyes look right on, and let thine eyelids look straight before thee. Ponder the path of thy feet, and let all thy ways be established. Turn not to the right hand nor to the left: remove thy foot from evil.

Proverbs 4:23−27

Giving all diligence, add to your faith virtue; and to virtue, knowledge; and to knowledge, temperance; and to temperance, patience; and to patience, godliness; and to godliness, brotherly kindness; and to brotherly kindness, charity. For if these things be in you, and abound, they make you that ye shall neither be barren nor unfruitful in the knowledge of our Lord Jesus Christ.

2 Peter 1:5−8

Keep thy tongue from evil,
and thy lips from speaking guile.

Psalm 34:13

He that will love life, and see good days, let him refrain his tongue from evil, and his lips that they speak no guile.

1 Peter 3:10

Now ye also put off all these; anger, wrath, malice, blasphemy, filthy communication out of your mouth.

Colossians 3:8

Flee also youthful lusts: but follow righteousness, faith, charity, peace, with them that call on the Lord out of a pure heart.

2 Timothy 2:22

Abhor that which is evil; cleave to that which is good.

Romans 12:9

Trust in the Lord, and do good;
so shalt thou dwell in the land, and verily thou
    shalt be fed.
Delight thyself also in the Lord;
and he shall give thee the desires of thine heart.

Commit thy way unto the Lord;
trust also in him; and he shall bring it to pass.
And he shall bring forth thy righteousness as the
    light,
and thy judgment as the noonday.

Rest in the Lord, and wait patiently for him:
fret not thyself because of him who prospereth
    in his way,
because of the man who bringeth wicked devices
    to pass.

Cease from anger, and forsake wrath:
fret not thyself in any wise to do evil.

Psalm 37:3−8

Fear God.

1 Peter 2:17

Blessed is the man that feareth the Lord,
that delighteth greatly in his commandments.
His seed shall be mighty upon earth:
the generation of the upright shall be
    blessed.

Psalm 112:1, 2

DISCIPLES

Disciples

The Lord hath anointed me to preach good tidings unto the meek; he hath sent me to bind up the broken-hearted, to proclaim liberty to the captives, and the opening of the prison to them that are bound; to proclaim the acceptable year of the Lord, and the day of vengeance of our God; to comfort all that mourn; to appoint unto them that mourn in Zion, to give unto them beauty for ashes, the oil of joy for mourning, the garment of praise for the spirit of heaviness.

Isaiah 61:1−3

Jesus came into Galilee, preaching the gospel of the kingdom of God, and saying, The time is fulfilled, and the kingdom of God is at hand: repent ye, and believe the gospel.

Mark 1:14, 15

My doctrine is not mine, but his that sent me. If any man will do his will, he shall know of the doctrine, whether it be of God, or whether I speak of myself.

John 7:16, 17

Choose you this day whom ye will serve; . . . as for me and my house, we will serve the Lord.

Joshua 24:15

Commit thy works unto the Lord, and thy thoughts shall be established.

Proverbs 16:3

[Jesus] said unto them, Go ye into all the world, and preach the gospel to every creature. He that believeth and is baptized shall be saved; but he that believeth not shall be damned. And these signs shall follow them that believe; In my name shall they cast out devils; they shall speak with new tongues; they shall take up serpents; and if they drink any deadly thing, it shall not hurt them; they shall lay hands on the sick, and they shall recover.

Mark 16:15−18

All that the Father giveth me shall come to me; and him that cometh to me I will in no wise cast out.

John 6:37

If any man serve me, let him follow me; and where I am, there shall also my servant be: if any man serve me, him will my Father honor.

John 12:26

Ye are my friends, if ye do whatsoever I command you. Henceforth I call you not servants; for the servant knoweth not what his lord doeth: but I have called you friends; for all things that I have heard of my Father I have made known unto you.

John 15:14, 15

Train up a child in the way he should go: and when he is old, he will not depart from it.

Proverbs 22:6

The secret things belong unto the Lord our God: but those things which are revealed belong unto us and to our children for ever, that we may do all the words of this law.

Deuteronomy 29:29

Ye fathers, provoke not your children to wrath: but bring them up in the nurture and admonition of the Lord.

Ephesians 6:4

As every man hath receiveth the gift, even so minister the same one to another, as good stewards of the manifold grace of God.

1 Peter 4:10

Walk worthy of the vocation wherewith ye are called.

Ephesians 4:1

I will instruct thee and teach thee
in the way which thou shalt go:
I will guide thee with mine eye.

Psalm 32:8

Thine eyes shall see thy teachers: and thine ears shall hear a word behind thee, saying, This is the way, walk ye in it, when ye turn to the right hand, and when ye turn to the left.

Isaiah 30:20, 21

Be not conformed to this world: but be ye transformed by the renewing of your mind, that ye may prove what is that good, and acceptable, and perfect will of God.

Romans 12:2

He that receiveth you receiveth me; and he that receiveth me receiveth him that sent me.

Matthew 10:40

Behold, I send you forth as sheep in the midst of wolves: be ye therefore wise as serpents, and harmless as doves.

Matthew 10:16

In the sweat of thy face shalt thou eat bread.

Genesis 3:19

Give not that which is holy unto the dogs, neither cast ye your pearls before swine, lest they trample them under their feet, and turn again and rend you.

Matthew 7:6

Be ye doers of the word, and not hearers only, deceiving your own selves.

James 1:22

All power is given unto me in heaven and in earth. Go ye therefore, and teach all nations, baptizing them in the name of the Father, and of the Son, and of the Holy Ghost: teaching them to observe all things whatsoever I have commanded you: and, lo, I am with you alway, even unto the end of the world.

Matthew 28:18–20

Verily, verily, I say unto you, He that believeth on me, the works that I do shall he do also; and greater works than these shall he do; because I go unto my Father.

John 14:12

Therefore, my beloved brethren, be ye steadfast, unmovable, always abounding in the work of the Lord, forasmuch as ye know that your labor is not in vain in the Lord.

1 Corinthians 15:58

For it is God which worketh in you both to will and to do of his good pleasure.

Philippians 2:13

If we walk in the light, as he is in the light, we have fellowship one with another.

1 John 1:7

Thou art Peter . . . . And I will give unto thee the keys of the kingdom of heaven: and whatsoever thou shalt bind on earth shall be bound in heaven; and whatsoever thou shalt loose on earth shall be loosed in heaven.

Matthew 16:18, 19

———

Then spake Jesus again unto them, saying, I am the light of the world: he that followeth me shall not walk in darkness, but shall have the light of life.

John 8:12

———

For God is not unrighteous to forget your work and labor of love, which ye have showed toward his name, in that ye have ministered to the saints, and do minister.

Hebrews 6:10

FAITH
FORGIVENESS

Faith

Who hath ascended up into heaven, or descended? Who hath gathered the wind in his fists? Who hath bound the waters in a garment? Who hath established all the ends of the earth? What is his name, and what is his son's name, if thou canst tell?

Proverbs 30:4

I am Alpha and Omega, the beginning and the end, the first and the last.

Revelation 22:13

I am the Lord, I change not.

Malachi 3:6

There is no power but of God.

Romans 13:1

There is but one God.

1 Corinthians 8:6

Without faith it is impossible to please him: for he that cometh to God must believe that he is, and that he is a rewarder of them that diligently seek him.

Hebrews 11:6

And Jesus answering saith unto them, Have faith in God. For verily I say unto you, That whosoever shall say unto this mountain, Be thou removed, and be thou cast into the sea; and shall not doubt in his heart, but shall believe that those things which he saith shall come to pass; he shall have whatsoever he saith. Therefore I say unto you, What things soever ye desire, when ye pray, believe that ye receive them, and ye shall have them.

Mark 11:22–24

Now faith is the substance of things hoped for, the evidence of things not seen. Through faith we understand that the worlds were framed by the word of God, so that things which are seen were not made of things which do appear.

Hebrews 11:1, 3

For thus saith the Lord unto the house of Israel, Seek ye me, and ye shall live.

Amos 5:4

I am not ashamed of the gospel of Christ: for it is the power of God unto salvation to every one that believeth.

Romans 1:16

Let not your heart be troubled: ye believe in God, believe also in me.

John 14:1

Search the Scriptures; for in them ye think ye have eternal life: and they are they which testify of me. And ye will not come to me, that ye might have life. I receive not honor from men. But I know you, that ye have not the love of God in you. I am come in my Father's name, and ye receive me not: if another shall come in his own name, him ye will receive. How can ye believe, which receive honor one of another, and seek not the honor that cometh from God only? Do not think that I will accuse you to the Father: there is one that accuseth you, even Moses, in whom ye trust.

John 5:39−45

All things are possible to him that believeth.

Mark 9:23

When I was a child, I spake as a child, I understood as a child, I thought as a child: but when I became a man, I put away childish things.

1 Corinthians 13:11

Jesus saith . . . I am the way, the truth, and the life: no man cometh unto the Father, but by me.

John 14:6

Behold, I have set before thee an open door, and no man can shut it.

Revelation 3:8

Beloved, believe not every spirit, but try the spirits whether they are of God: because many false prophets are gone out into the world. Hereby know ye the Spirit of God: Every spirit that confesseth that Jesus Christ is come in the flesh is of God: and every spirit that confesseth not that Jesus Christ is come in the flesh is not of God. . . . Ye are of God, little children, and have overcome them: because greater is he that is in you, than he that is in the world.

1 John 4:1−4

He that is not with me is against me; and he that gathereth not with me scattereth abroad.

Matthew 12:30

According to your faith be it unto you.

Matthew 9:29

Therefore whosoever heareth these sayings of mine, and doeth them, I will liken him unto a wise man, which built his house upon a rock: and the rain descended, and the floods came, and the winds blew, and beat upon that house; and it fell not: for it was founded upon a rock.

Matthew 7:24, 25

We walk by faith, not by sight.

2 Corinthians 5:7

What doth it profit, my brethren, though a man say he hath faith, and have not works? can faith save him? Yea, a man may say, Thou hast faith, and I have works: show me thy faith without thy works, and I will show thee my faith by my works. For as the body without the spirit is dead, so faith without works is dead also.

James 2:14, 18, 26

═══

The just shall live by faith.

Romans 1:17

═══

It is expedient for you that I go away: for if I go not away, the Comforter will not come unto you; but if I depart, I will send him unto you.

John 16:7

═══

Ye have heard how I said unto you, I go away, and come again unto you. If ye loved me, ye would rejoice, because I said, I go unto the Father: for my Father is greater than I.

John 14:28

═══

No man can come to me, except the Father which hath sent me draw him: and I will raise him up at the last day.

John 6:44

Then came Jesus, the doors being shut, and stood in the midst, and said, Peace be unto you. Then saith he to Thomas, Reach hither thy finger, and behold my hands; and reach hither thy hand, and thrust it into my side; and be not faithless, but believing. And Thomas answered and said unto him, My Lord and my God. Jesus saith unto him, Thomas, because thou hast seen me, thou hast believed: blessed are they that have not seen, and yet have believed.

John 20:26–29

Jesus said unto her, I am the resurrection, and the life: he that believeth in me, though he were dead, yet shall he live: and whosoever liveth and believeth in me shall never die.

John 11:25, 26

We are saved by hope: but hope that is seen is not hope: for what a man seeth, why doth he yet hope for? But if we hope for that we see not, then do we with patience wait for it.

Romans 8:24, 25

Believe on the Lord Jesus Christ, and thou shalt be saved, and thy house.

Acts 16:31

Heaven and earth shall pass away, but my words shall not pass away.

Matthew 24:35

Verily, verily, I say unto you, He that believeth on me hath everlasting life. I am that bread of life. Your fathers did eat manna in the wilderness, and are dead. This is the bread which cometh down from heaven, that a man may eat thereof, and not die. I am the living bread which came down from heaven: if any man eat of this bread, he shall live for ever: and the bread that I will give is my flesh, which I will give for the life of the world.

John 6:47−51

Verily, verily, I say unto you, He that heareth my word, and believeth on him that sent me, hath everlasting life, and shall not come into condemnation; but is passed from death unto life.

John 5:24

If thou shalt confess with thy mouth the Lord Jesus, and shalt believe in thine heart that God hath raised him from the dead, thou shalt be saved. For with the heart man believeth unto righteousness; and with the mouth confession is made unto salvation.

Romans 10:9, 10

Verily, verily, I say unto thee, Except a man be born again, he cannot see the kingdom of God.

John 3:3

Thy faith hath saved thee; go in peace.

Luke 7:50

Forgiveness

If thou bring thy gift to the altar, and there rememberest that thy brother hath aught against thee; leave there thy gift before the altar, and go thy way; first be reconciled to thy brother, and then come and offer thy gift.

Matthew 5:23, 24

Bless them which persecute you: bless, and curse not.

Romans 12:14

[Be ye] not rendering evil for evil, or railing for railing: but contrariwise blessing; knowing that ye are thereunto called, that ye should inherit a blessing.

1 Peter 3:9

Be not hasty in thy spirit to be angry: for anger resteth in the bosom of fools.

Ecclesiastes 7:9

Pray for them which despitefully use you, and persecute you.

Matthew 5:44

When ye stand praying, forgive, if ye have aught against any.

Mark 11:25

Ye have heard that it hath been said, An eye for an eye, and a tooth for a tooth: but I say unto you, That ye resist not evil: but whosoever shall smite thee on thy right cheek, turn to him the other also. And if any man will sue thee at the law, and take away thy coat, let him have thy cloak also. And whosoever shall compel thee to go a mile, go with him twain. Give to him that asketh thee, and from him that would borrow of thee turn not thou away.

Matthew 5:38–42

If thy brother trespass against thee, rebuke him; and if he repent, forgive him. And if he trespass against thee seven times in a day, and seven times in a day turn again to thee, saying, I repent; thou shalt forgive him.

Luke 17:3, 4

Judge not, and ye shall not be judged: condemn not, and ye shall not be condemned: forgive, and ye shall be forgiven.

Luke 6:37

If ye forgive men their trespasses, your heavenly Father will also forgive you: but if ye forgive not men their trespasses, neither will your Father forgive your trespasses.

Matthew 6:14, 15

He shall have judgment without mercy, that hath showed no mercy.

James 2:13

For if ye love them which love you, what thank have ye? for sinners also love those that love them. And if ye do good to them which do good to you, what thank have ye? for sinners also do even the same. And if ye lend to them of whom ye hope to receive, what thank have ye? for sinners also lend to sinners, to receive as much again. But love ye your enemies, and do good, and lend, hoping for nothing again; and your reward shall be great, and ye shall be the children of the Highest: for he is kind unto the unthankful and to the evil. Be ye therefore merciful, as your Father also is merciful.

Luke 6:32−36

Be ye kind one to another, tender-hearted, forgiving one another, even as God for Christ's sake hath forgiven you.

Ephesians 4:32

Watch therefore; for ye know not what hour your Lord doth come.

Matthew 24:42

He that covereth his sins shall not prosper: but whoso confesseth and forsaketh them shall have mercy.

Proverbs 28:13

Are not two sparrows sold for a farthing? and one of them shall not fall on the ground without your Father. But the very hairs of your head are all numbered. Fear ye not therefore, ye are of more value than many sparrows. Whosoever therefore shall confess me before men, him will I confess also before my Father which is in heaven. But whosoever shall deny me before men, him will I also deny before my Father which is in heaven.

Matthew 10:29–33

If my people, which are called by my name, shall humble themselves, and pray, and seek my face, and turn from their wicked ways; then will I hear from heaven, and will forgive their sin, and will heal their land.

2 Chronicles 7:14

How think ye? if a man have a hundred sheep, and one of them be gone astray, doth he not leave the ninety and nine, and goeth into the mountains, and seeketh that which is gone astray? And if so be that he find it, verily I say unto you, he rejoiceth more of that sheep, than of the ninety and nine which went not astray. Even so it is not the will of your Father which is in heaven, that one of these little ones should perish.

Matthew 18:12–14

Who is he that condemneth? It is Christ that died, yea rather, that is risen again, who is even at the right hand of God, who also maketh intercession for us.

Romans 8:34

And it came to pass, as Jesus sat at meat in the house, behold, many publicans and sinners came and sat down with him and his disciples. And when the Pharisees saw it, they said unto his disciples, Why eateth your master with publicans and sinners? But when Jesus heard that, he said unto them, They that be whole need not a physician, but they that are sick. But go ye and learn what that meaneth, I will have mercy, and not sacrifice: for I am not come to call the righteous, but sinners to repentance.

Matthew 9:10−13

Joy shall be in heaven over one sinner that repenteth, more than over ninety and nine just persons, which need no repentance.

Luke 15:7

I have blotted out, as a thick cloud, thy transgressions, and, as a cloud, thy sins: return unto me; for I have redeemed thee.

Isaiah 44:22

And Abraham drew near, and said, Wilt thou also destroy the righteous with the wicked? Peradventure there be fifty righteous within the city: wilt thou also destroy and not spare the place for the fifty righteous that are therein? . . . Shall not the Judge of all the earth do right? And the Lord said, If I find in Sodom fifty righteous within the city, then I will spare all the place for their sakes.

Genesis 18:23−26

160

Seest thou this woman? I entered into thine house, thou gavest me no water for my feet: but she hath washed my feet with tears, and wiped them with the hairs of her head. Thou gavest me no kiss: but this woman, since the time I came in, hath not ceased to kiss my feet. My head with oil thou didst not anoint: but this woman hath anointed my feet with ointment. Wherefore I say unto thee, Her sins, which are many, are forgiven; for she loved much: but to whom little is forgiven, the same loveth little.

Luke 7:44–47

Therefore is the kingdom of heaven likened unto a certain king, which would take account of his servants. And when he had begun to reckon, one was brought unto him, which owed him ten thousand talents. But forasmuch as he had not to pay, his lord commanded him to be sold, and his wife, and children, and all that he had, and payment to be made. The servant therefore fell down, and worshipped him, saying, Lord, have patience with me, and I will pay thee all. Then the lord of that servant was moved with compassion, and loosed him, and forgave him the dept.

Matthew 18:23–27

Samuel said unto the people, Fear not: ye have done all this wickedness: yet turn not aside from following the Lord, but serve the Lord with all your heart. For the Lord will not forsake his people for his great name's sake: because it hath pleased the Lord to make you his people.

1 Samuel 12:20, 22

Let not thine hands be slack. The Lord thy God in the midst of thee is mighty; he will save, he will rejoice over thee with joy; he will rest in his love, he will joy over thee with singing.

Zephaniah 3:16, 17

God standeth in the congregation of
  the mighty;
he judgeth among the gods.

Psalm 82:1

O God, thou knowest my foolishness;
and my sins are not hid from thee.

Psalm 69:5

[The Lord] forgiveth all thine iniquities;
. . . healeth all thy diseases.

Psalm 103:3

The Lord is not slack concerning his promise, as some men count slackness; but is long-suffering to us-ward, not willing that any should perish, but that all should come to repentance.

2 Peter 3:9

Who shall lay any thing to the charge of God's elect? It is God that justifieth.

Romans 8:33

Rend your heart, and not your garments, and turn unto the Lord your God: for he is gracious and merciful, slow to anger, and of great kindness, and repenteth him of the evil.

Joel 2:13

The Lord seeth not as man seeth; for man looketh on the outward appearance, but the Lord looketh on the heart.

1 Samuel 16:7

Who is a God like unto thee, that pardoneth iniquity, and passeth by the transgression of the remnant of his heritage? he retaineth not his anger for ever, because he delighteth in mercy.

Micah 7:18

Have I any pleasure at all that the wicked should die? saith the Lord God: and not that he should return from his ways, and live?

Ezekiel 18:23

It is of God's mercies that we are not consumed, because his compassions fail not. They are new every morning: great is thy faithfulness.

Lamentations 3:22, 23

The blood of Jesus Christ his Son cleanseth us from all sin.

1 John 1:7

But God commendeth his love toward us, in that, while we were yet sinners, Christ died for us.

Romans 5:8

HUMILITY
HYPOCRISY

Humility

Two men went up into the temple to pray; the one a Pharisee, and the other a publican. The Pharisee stood and prayed thus with himself, God, I thank thee, that I am not as other men are, extortioners, unjust, adulterers, or even as this publican. I fast twice in the week, I give tithes of all that I possess. And the publican, standing afar off, would not lift up so much as his eyes unto heaven, but smote upon his breast, saying, God be merciful to me a sinner. I tell you, this man went down to his house justified rather than the other: for every one that exalteth himself shall be abased; and he that humbleth himself shall be exalted.

Luke 18:10−14

Be clothed with humility: for God resisteth the proud, and giveth grace to the humble. Humble yourselves therefore under the mighty hand of God, that he may exalt you in due time.

1 Peter 5:5, 6

Beware of the scribes, which desire to walk in long robes, and love greetings in the markets, and the highest seats in the synagogues, and the chief rooms at feasts; which devour widows' houses, and for a show make long prayers.

Luke 20:46−47

The tongue is a little member, and boasteth great things. Behold, how great a matter a little fire kindleth! . . . The tongue also is a fire. . . .

James 3:5, 6

Pride goeth before destruction, and a haughty spirit before a fall.

Proverbs 16:18

The backslider in heart shall be filled with his own ways: and a good man shall be satisfied from himself.

Proverbs 14:14

Whoso keepeth his mouth and his tongue, keepeth his soul from troubles.

Proverbs 21:23

Talk no more so exceeding proudly; let not arrogancy come out of your mouth: for the Lord is a God of knowledge, and by him actions are weighed.

1 Samuel 2:3

Woe unto them that are wise in their own eyes, and prudent in their own sight!

Isaiah 5:21

There was a certain rich man, which was clothed in purple and fine linen, and fared sumptuously every day: and there was a certain beggar named Lazarus, which was laid at his gate, full of sores, and desiring to be fed with the crumbs which fell from the rich man's table: moreover the dogs came and licked his sores. And it came to pass, that the beggar died, and was carried by the angels into Abraham's bosom: the rich man also died, and was buried; and in hell he lifted up his eyes, being in torments, and seeth Abraham afar off, and Lazarus in his bosom. And he cried and said, Father Abraham, have mercy on me, and send Lazarus, that he may dip the tip of his finger in water, and cool my tongue; for I am tormented in this flame.

Luke 16:19−24

By humility and the fear of the Lord are riches, and honor, and life.

Proverbs 22:4

Beware that thou forget not the Lord thy God, . . . [lest] thou say in thine heart, My power and the might of mine hand hath gotten me this wealth. But thou shalt remember the Lord thy God: for it is he that giveth thee power to get wealth, that he may establish his covenant which he sware unto thy fathers, as it is this day.

Deuteronomy 8:11, 17, 18

Likewise, ye younger, submit yourselves unto the elder. Yea, all of you be subject one to another, and be clothed with humility: for God resisteth the proud, but giveth grace to the humble.

1 Peter 5:5

Put . . . in mind to be subject to principalities and powers, to obey magistrates, to be ready to every good work, to speak evil of no man, to be no brawlers, but gentle, showing all meekness unto all men.

Titus 3:1, 2

Mind not high things, but condescend to men of low estate. Be not wise in your own conceits.

Romans 12:16

Ye shall not respect persons in judgment; but ye shall hear the small as well as the great; ye shall not be afraid of the face of man; for the judgment is God's.

Deuteronomy 1:17

Whosoever therefore shall humble himself as this little child, the same is greatest in the kingdom of heaven. And whoso shall receive one such little child in my name receiveth me.

Matthew 18:4, 5

Whosoever shall exalt himself shall be abased; and he that shall humble himself shall be exalted.

Matthew 23:12

I had rather be a doorkeeper in the
  house of my God,
than to dwell in the tents of wickedness.

Psalm 84:10

Hypocrisy

When thou prayest, thou shalt not be as the hypocrites are: for they love to pray standing in the synagogues and in the corners of the streets, that they may be seen of men. Verily I say unto you, They have their reward. But thou, when thou prayest, enter into thy closet, and when thou hast shut thy door, pray to thy Father which is in secret; and thy Father which seeth in secret shall reward thee openly.

Matthew 6:5, 6

Either make the tree good, and his fruit good; or else make the tree corrupt, and his fruit corrupt: for the tree is known by his fruit. A good man out of the good treasure of the heart bringeth forth good things: and an evil man out of the evil treasure bringeth forth evil things.

Matthew 12:33, 35

The scribes and the Pharisees sit in Moses' seat: all therefore whatsoever they bid you observe, that observe and do; but do not ye after their works: for they say, and do not.

Matthew 23:2, 3

A double-minded man is unstable in all his ways.

James 1:8

Woe unto you, scribes and Pharisees, hypocrites! for ye pay tithe of mint and anise and cummin, and have omitted the weightier matters of the law, judgment, mercy, and faith: those ought ye to have done, and not to leave the other undone. Ye blind guides, which strain at a gnat, and swallow a camel.

Matthew 23:23, 24

Why beholdest thou the mote that is in thy brother's eye, but considereth not the beam that is in thine own eye? Thou hypocrite, first cast out the beam out of thine own eye; and then shalt thou see clearly to cast out the mote out of thy brother's eye.

Matthew 7:3, 5

For there is no faithfulness in their mouth;
their inward part is very wickedness;
their throat is an open sepulchre;
they flatter with their tongue.

Psalm 5:9

I say unto you, That every idle word that men shall speak, they shall give account thereof in the day of judgment. For by thy words thou shalt be justified, and by thy words thou shalt be condemned.

Matthew 12:36, 37

Woe unto you, scribes and Pharisees, hypocrites! for ye make clean the outside of the cup and of the platter, but within they are full of extortion and excess. Thou blind Pharisee, cleanse first that which is within the cup and platter, that the outside of them may be clean also. Woe unto you, scribes and Pharisees, hypocrites! for ye are like unto whited sepulchres, which indeed appear beautiful outward, but are within full of dead men's bones, and of all uncleanness. Even so ye also outwardly appear righteous unto men, but within ye are full of hypocrisy and iniquity.

Matthew 23:25−28

Judge not according to the appearance, but judge righteous judgment.

John 7:24

Woe unto you also, ye lawyers! for ye lade men with burdens grievous to be borne, and ye yourselves touch not the burdens with one of your fingers.

Luke 11:46

Woe unto them that call evil good, and good evil; that put darkness for light, and light for darkness; and put bitter for sweet, and sweet for bitter!

Isaiah 5:20

Take heed that ye do not your alms before men, to be seen of them: otherwise ye have no reward of your Father which is in heaven. Therefore when thou doest thine alms, do not sound a trumpet before thee, as the hypocrites do in the synagogues and in the streets, that they may have glory of men. Verily I say unto you, They have their reward. But when thou doest alms, let not thy left hand know what thy right hand doeth: that thine alms may be in secret: and thy Father which seeth in secret himself shall reward thee openly.

Matthew 6:1−4

When ye fast, be not, as the hypocrites, of a sad countenance: for they disfigure their faces, that they may appear unto men to fast. Verily I say unto you, They have their reward. But thou, when thou fastest, anoint thine head, and wash thy face; that thou appear not unto men to fast, but unto thy Father which is in secret: and thy Father which seeth in secret shall reward thee openly.

Matthew 6:16−18

We ourselves also were sometime foolish, disobedient, deceived, serving divers lusts and pleasures, living in malice and envy, hateful, and hating one another. But after that the kindness and love of God our Saviour toward man appeared, not by works of righteousness which we have done, but according to his mercy he saved us, . . . these things I will that thou affirm constantly, that they which have believed in God might be careful to maintain good works.

Titus 3:3−5, 8

INSPIRATION

Inspiration

No prophecy of the Scripture is of any private interpretation. For the prophecy came not in old time by the will of man: but holy men of God spake as they were moved by the Holy Ghost.

2 Peter 1:20, 21

I will lead them in paths that they have not known: I will make darkness light before them, and crooked things straight. These things will I do unto them, and not forsake them.

Isaiah 42:16

Call unto me, and I will answer thee, and show thee great and mighty things, which thou knowest not.

Jeremiah 33:3

I send thee, to open their eyes, and to turn them from darkness to light, and from the power of Satan unto God.

Acts 26:17, 18

I will put my law in their inward parts, and write it in their hearts; and will be their God, and they shall be my people.

Jeremiah 31:33

It shall come to pass afterward, that I will pour out my Spirit upon all flesh; and your sons and your daughters shall prophesy, your old men shall dream dreams, your young men shall see visions.

Joel 2:28

For we are laborers together with God: ye are God's husbandry, ye are God's building.

1 Corinthians 3:9

Man shall not live by bread alone, but by every word that proceedeth out of the mouth of God.

Matthew 4:4

The heart of the wise teacheth his mouth, and addeth learning to his lips.

Proverbs 16:23

Out of the abundance of the heart the mouth speakest.

Matthew 12:34

Pleasant words are as a honeycomb, sweet to the soul, and health to the bones.

Proverbs 16:24

How beautiful upon the mountains are the feet of him that bringeth good tidings, that publisheth peace.

Isaiah 52:7

In the beginning was the Word, and the Word was with God, and the Word was God. The same was in the beginning with God. All things were made by him; and without him was not any thing made that was made. In him was life; and the life was the light of men. And the light shineth in darkness; and the darkness comprehended it not.

John 1:1−4

In quietness and in confidence shall be your strength.

Isaiah 30:15

When I sit in darkness, the Lord shall be a light unto me.

Micah 7:8

The people that walked in darkness have seen a great light: they that dwell in the land of the shadow of death, upon them hath the light shined.

Isaiah 9:2

Light is come into the world, and men loved darkness rather than light, because their deeds were evil. For every one that doeth evil hateth the light, neither cometh to the light, lest his deeds should be reproved. But he that doeth truth cometh to the light, that his deeds may be made manifest, that they are wrought in God.

John 3:19−21

My sheep hear my voice, and I know them, and they follow me: and I give unto them eternal life; and they shall never perish, neither shall any man pluck them out of my hand. My Father, which gave them me, is greater than all; and no man is able to pluck them out of the Father's hand. I and my Father are one.

John 10:27—30

Walk while ye have the light, lest darkness come upon you.

John 12:35

Whosoever drinketh of this water shall thirst again: but whosoever drinketh of the water that I shall give him shall never thirst; but the water that I shall give him shall be in him a well of water springing up into everlasting life.

John 4:13, 14

For this God is our God for ever and ever:
he will be our guide even unto death.

Psalm 48:14

The Lord openeth the eyes of the blind:
the Lord raiseth them that are bowed down.

Psalm 146:8

Thy word is a lamp unto my feet,
and a light unto my path.

Psalm 119:105

How precious also are thy thoughts
    unto me, O God!
How great is the sum of them!
If I should count them, they are more
    in number than the sand:
when I awake, I am still with thee.

Psalm 139:17, 18

O the depth of the riches both of the wisdom and knowledge of God! how unsearchable are his judgments, and his ways past finding out!

Romans 11:33

When the Comforter is come, whom I will send unto you from the Father, even the Spirit of truth, which proceedeth from the Father, he shall testify of me.

John 15:26

All flesh is grass, and all the goodliness thereof is as the flower of the field.

Isaiah 40:6

For God hath not given us the spirit of fear; but of power, and of love, and of a sound mind.

2 Timothy 1:7

With God nothing shall be impossible.

Luke 1:37

The law of the Lord is perfect,
converting the soul:
the testimony of the Lord is sure,
making wise the simple.
The statutes of the Lord are right,
rejoicing the heart:
the commandment of the Lord is pure,
enlightening the eyes.

Psalm 19:7, 8

I am crucified with Christ: nevertheless I live; yet not I, but Christ liveth in me: and the life which I now live in the flesh I live by the faith of the Son of God, who loved me, and gave himself for me.

Galatians 2:20

Where there is no vision, the people perish.

Proverbs 29:18

JUDGMENT

Judgment

None of us liveth to himself, and no man dieth to himself. For whether we live, we live unto the Lord; and whether we die, we die unto the Lord: whether we live therefore, or die, we are the Lord's. So then every one of us shall give account of himself to God. Let us not therefore judge one another any more.

Romans 14:7, 8, 12, 13

Marriage is honorable in all, and the bed undefiled: but whoremongers and adulterers God will judge.

Hebrews 13:4

Thy money perish with thee, because thou hast thought that the gift of God may be purchased with money.

Acts 8:20

Vengeance is mine; I will repay, saith the Lord. Therefore if thine enemy hunger, feed him; if he thirst, give him drink: for in so doing thou shalt heap coals of fire on his head.

Romans 12:19, 20

A soft answer turneth away wrath: but grievous words stir up anger.

Proverbs 15:1

The fear of the Lord is clean,
enduring for ever:
the judgments of the Lord are true
and righteous altogether.
More to be desired are they than gold.

Psalm 19:9, 10

Recompense to no man evil for evil.

Romans 12:17

It is Christ that died, yea rather, that is risen again, who is even at the right hand of God, who also maketh intercession for us.

Romans 8:34

Happy is the man whom God correcteth: therefore despise not thou the chastening of the Almighty: for he maketh sore, and bindeth up: he woundeth, and his hands make whole.

Job 5:17, 18

Now no chastening for the present seemeth to be joyous, but grievous: nevertheless, afterward it yieldeth the peaceable fruit of righteousness unto them which are exercised thereby.

Hebrews 12:11

My son, despise not the chastening of the Lord; neither be weary of his correction: for whom the Lord loveth he correcteth; even as a father the son in whom he delighteth.

Proverbs 3:11, 12

For a small moment have I forsaken thee; but with great mercies will I gather thee. In a little wrath I hid my face from thee for a moment; but with everlasting kindness will I have mercy on thee, saith the Lord thy Redeemer.

Isaiah 54:7, 8

Whom the Lord loveth he chasteneth, and scourgeth every son whom he receiveth.

Hebrews 12:6

If ye endure chastening, God dealeth with you as with sons.

Hebrews 12:7

He that spareth his rod hateth his son: but he that loveth him chasteneth him betimes.

Proverbs 13:24

If any would not work, neither should he eat.

2 Thessalonians 3:10

All they that take the sword shall perish with the sword.

Matthew 26:52

The wages of sin is death.

Romans 6:23

He that believeth on the Son hath everlasting life: and he that believeth not the Son shall not see life; but the wrath of God abideth on him.

John 3:36

God will not cast away a perfect man, neither will he help the evildoer.

Job 8:20

He maketh his sun to rise on the evil and on the good, and sendeth rain on the just and on the unjust.

Matthew 5:45

For the Lord loveth judgment,
and forsaketh not his saints;
they are preserved for ever.

Psalm 37:28

The Lord preserveth all them that love him:
but all the wicked will he destroy.

Psalm 145:20

I said in mine heart, God shall judge the righteous and the wicked: for there is a time there for every purpose and for every work.

Ecclesiastes 3:17

The wicked are like the troubled sea, when it cannot rest, whose waters cast up mire and dirt. There is no peace, saith my God, to the wicked.

Isaiah 57:20, 21

———

The memory of the just is blessed: but the name of the wicked shall rot.

Proverbs 10:7

———

The wicked shall be turned into hell,
and all the nations that forget God.

Psalm 9:17

KINGDOM OF GOD
KNOWLEDGE

Kingdom of God

When the Son of man shall come in his glory, and all the holy angels with him, then shall he sit upon the throne of his glory: and before him shall be gathered all nations: and he shall separate them one from another, as a shepherd divideth his sheep from the goats: and he shall set the sheep on his right hand, but the goats on the left. Then shall the King say unto them on his right hand, Come, ye blessed of my Father, inherit the kingdom prepared for you from the foundation of the world: for I was ahungered, and ye gave me meat: I was thirsty, and ye gave me drink: I was a stranger, and ye took me in: naked, and ye clothed me: I was sick, and ye visited me: I was in prison, and ye came unto me. Then shall the righteous answer him, saying, Lord, when saw we thee ahungered, and fed thee? or thirsty, and gave thee drink? When saw we thee a stranger, and took thee in? or naked, and clothed thee? Or when saw we thee sick, or in prison, and came unto thee? And the King shall answer and say unto them, Verily I say unto you, Inasmuch as ye have done it unto one of the least of these my brethren, ye have done it unto me.

Matthew 25:31−40

In my Father's house are many mansions: if it were not so, I would have told you. I go to prepare a place for you. And if I go and prepare a place for you, I will come again, and receive you unto myself; that where I am, there ye may be also.

John 14:2, 3

The earth is the Lord's, and the
    fulness thereof;
the world, and they that dwell therein.
For he hath founded it upon the seas,
and established it upon the floods.

Who shall ascend into the hill of the Lord?
Or who shall stand in his holy place?
He that hath clean hands, and a pure heart;
who hath not lifted up his soul unto vanity,
nor sworn deceitfully.

Psalm 24:1—4

Arise, shine; for thy light is come, and the glory of the Lord is
risen upon thee. For, behold, the darkness shall cover the
earth, and gross darkness the people: but the Lord shall arise
upon thee, and his glory shall be seen upon thee.

Isaiah 60:1, 2

Lord, who shall abide in thy tabernacle?
Who shall dwell in thy holy hill?

He that walketh uprightly, and worketh
    righteousness,
and speaketh the truth in his heart.

Psalm 15:1, 2

Know ye not that the unrighteous shall not inherit the kingdom of God? Be not deceived: neither fornicators, nor idolaters, nor adulterers, nor effeminate, nor abusers of themselves with mankind, nor thieves, nor covetous, nor drunkards, nor revilers, nor extortioners, shall inherit the kingdom of God. And such were some of you: but ye are washed, but ye are sanctified, but ye are justified in the name of Lord Jesus, and by the Spirit of our God.

1 Corinthians 6:9−11

The dead in Christ shall rise first: then we which are alive and remain shall be caught up together with them in the clouds, to meet the Lord in the air: and so shall we ever be with the Lord.

1 Thessalonians 4:16, 17

The meek shall inherit the earth;
and shall delight themselves in the abundance
   of peace.

Psalm 37:11

They shall come from the east, and from the west, and from the north, and from the south, and shall sit down in the kingdom of God. And, behold, there are last which shall be first; and there are first which shall be last.

Luke 13:29, 30

Hearken, my beloved brethren, Hath not God chosen the poor of this world rich in faith, and heirs of the kingdom which he hath promised to them that love him? But ye have despised the poor.

James 2:5, 6

Not every one that saith unto me, Lord, Lord, shall enter into the kingdom of heaven; but he that doeth the will of my Father which is in heaven.

Matthew 7:21

No man, having put his hand to the plow, and looking back, is fit for the kingdom of God.

Luke 9:62

The Lord was ready to save me: therefore we will sing my songs to the stringed instruments all the days of our life in the house of the Lord.

Isaiah 38:20

And it shall be said in that day, Lo, this is our God; we have waited for him, . . . we will be glad and rejoice in his salvation.

Isaiah 25:9

As he sat upon the mount of Olives, the disciples came unto him privately, saying, Tell us, when shall these things be? and what shall be the sign of thy coming, and of the end of the world? And Jesus answered and said unto them, Take heed that no man deceive you. For nation shall rise against nation, and kingdom against kingdom: and there shall be famines, and pestilences, and earthquakes, in divers places. All these are the beginning of sorrows. And then shall many be offended, and shall betray one another, and shall hate one another. And because iniquity shall abound, the love of many shall wax cold. But he that shall endure unto the end, the same shall be saved. And this gospel of the kingdom shall be preached in all the world for a witness unto all nations; and then shall the end come.

Matthew 24:3, 4, 7, 8, 10, 12–14

The Lord knoweth the days of the upright:
and their inheritance shall be for ever.

Psalm 37:18

Again, the kingdom of heaven is like unto a net, that was cast into the sea, and gathered of every kind: which, when it was full, they drew to shore, and sat down, and gathered the good into vessels, but cast the bad away. So shall it be at the end of the world: the angels shall come forth, and sever the wicked from among the just, and shall cast them into the furnace of fire: there shall be wailing and gnashing of teeth.

Matthew 13:47–50

There shall be signs in the sun, and in the moon, and in the stars; and upon the earth distress of nations, with perplexity; the sea and the waves roaring; men's hearts failing them for fear, and for looking after those things which are coming on the earth: for the powers of heaven shall be shaken. And then shall they see the Son of man coming in a cloud with power and great glory. And when these things begin to come to pass, then look up, and lift up your heads; for your redemption draweth nigh.

Luke 21:25−28

I will show wonders in the heavens and in the earth, blood, and fire, and pillars of smoke. The sun shall be turned into darkness, and the moon into blood, before the great and terrible day of the Lord come. And it shall come to pass, that whosoever shall call on the name of the Lord shall be delivered.

Joel 2:30−32

I appoint unto you a kingdom, as my Father hath appointed unto me; that ye may eat and drink at my table in my kingdom, and sit on thrones judging the twelve tribes of Israel.

Luke 22:29, 30

But will God indeed dwell on the earth? behold, the heaven and heaven of heavens cannot contain thee; how much less this house that I have builded?

1 Kings 8:27

And, Thou, Lord, in the beginning hast laid the foundation of the earth; and the heavens are the works of thine hands. They shall perish, but thou remainest: and they all shall wax old as doth a garment; and as a vesture shalt thou fold them up, and they shall be changed: but thou art the same, and thy years shall not fail.

Hebrews 1:10−12

This same Jesus, which is taken up from you into heaven, shall so come in like manner as ye have seen him go into heaven.

Acts 1:11

And I saw a new heaven and a new earth: for the first heaven and the first earth were passed away; and there was no more sea. And I John saw the holy city, new Jerusalem, coming down from God out of heaven.

Revelation 21:1, 2

Beloved, be not ignorant of this one thing, that one day is with the Lord as a thousand years, and a thousand years as one day.

2 Peter 3:8

The heavens declare the glory of God;
and the firmament showeth his handiwork.

Psalm 19:1

Blessed be the God and Father of our Lord Jesus Christ, which according to his abundant mercy hath begotten us again unto a lively hope by the resurrection of Jesus Christ from the dead, to an inheritance incorruptible, and undefiled, and that fadeth not away, reserved in heaven for you.

1 Peter 1:3, 4

For God so loved the world, that he gave his only begotten Son, that whosoever believeth in him should not perish, but have everlasting life.

John 3:16

I have fought a good fight, I have finished my course, I have kept the faith: henceforth there is laid up for me a crown of righteousness, which the Lord, the righteous judge, shall give me at that day: and not to me only, but unto all them also that love his appearing.

2 Timothy 4:7, 8

One thing have I desired of the Lord,
that will I seek after;
that I may dwell in the house of
  the Lord
all the days of my life,
to behold the beauty of the Lord,
and to inquire in his temple.

Psalm 27:4

I know that my Redeemer liveth, and that he shall stand at the latter day upon the earth.

Job 19:25

Knowledge

The wisdom of this world is foolishness with God.

1 Corinthians 3:19

The fear of the Lord is the beginning of the wisdom: and the knowledge of the Holy is understanding. For by me thy days shall be multiplied, and the years of thy life shall be increased. If thou be wise, thou shalt be wise for thyself: but if thou scornest, thou alone shalt bear it.

Proverbs 9:10−12

All Scripture is given by inspiration of God, and is profitable for doctrine, for reproof, for correction, for instruction in righteousness: that the man of God may be perfect, thoroughly furnished unto all good works.

2 Timothy 3:16,17

Take my yoke upon you, and learn of me; for I am meek and lowly in heart: and ye shall find rest unto your souls.

Matthew 11:29

Through wisdom is a house builded; and by understanding it is established: and by knowledge shall the chambers be filled with all precious and pleasant riches.

Proverbs 24:3, 4

———

The price of wisdom is above rubies.

Job 28:18

———

Even a fool, when he holdeth his peace, is counted wise.

Proverbs 17:28

———

If the blind lead the blind, both shall fall into the ditch.

Matthew 15:14

———

The tongue of the wise useth knowledge aright: but the mouth of fools poureth out foolishness.

Proverbs 15:2

———

O foolish people, and without understanding; which have eyes, and see not; which have ears, and hear not.

Jeremiah 5:21

———

As the crackling of thorns under a pot, so is the laughter of the fool.

Ecclesiastes 7:6

When they therefore were come together, they asked of him, saying, Lord, wilt thou at this time restore again the kingdom of Israel? And he said unto them, It is not for you to know the times or the seasons, which the Father hath put in his own power. But ye shall receive power, after that the Holy Ghost is come upon you: and ye shall be witnesses unto me both in Jerusalem, and in all Judea, and in Samaria, and unto the uttermost part of the earth.

Acts 1:6−8

The fear of the Lord is the beginning of knowledge.

Proverbs 1:7

The Lord God hath given me the tongue of the learned, that I should know how to speak a word in season to him that is weary.

Isaiah 50:4

Behold, God is great, and we know him not, neither can the number of his years be searched out.

Job 36:26

Every man therefore that hath heard, and hath learned of the Father, cometh unto me.

John 6:45

Prove all things; hold fast that which is good.

1 Thessalonians 5:21

This I pray, that your love may abound yet more and more in knowledge and in all judgment; that ye may approve things that are excellent; that ye may be sincere and without offense till the day of Christ.

Philippians 1:9, 10

Study to show thyself approved unto God, a workman that needeth not to be ashamed, rightly dividing the word of truth.

2 Timothy 2:15

As newborn babes, desire the sincere milk of the word, that ye may grow thereby: if so be ye have tasted that the Lord is gracious.

1 Peter 2:2, 3

The word of God is quick, and powerful, and sharper than any two-edged sword, piercing even to the dividing asunder of soul and spirit, and of the joints and marrow, and is a discerner of the thoughts and intents of the heart.

Hebrews 4:12

The lip of truth shall be established for ever: but a lying tongue is but for a moment.

Proverbs 12:19

LOVE

Love

Though I speak with the tongues of men and angels, and have not charity, I am become as sounding brass, or a tinkling cymbal. And though I have the gift of prophecy, and understand all mysteries, and all knowledge; and though I have all faith, so that I could remove mountains, and have not charity, I am nothing. And though I bestow all my goods to feed the poor, and though I give my body to be burned, and have not charity, it profiteth me nothing. Charity suffereth long, and is kind; charity envieth not; charity vaunteth not itself, is not puffed up, doth not behave itself unseemly, seeketh not her own, is not easily provoked, thinketh no evil; rejoiceth not in iniquity, but rejoiceth in the truth; beareth all things, believeth all things, hopeth all things, endureth all things. Charity never faileth.

1 Corinthians 13:1-8

In all these things we are more than conquerors through him that loved us. For I am persuaded, that neither death, nor life, nor angels, nor principalities, nor powers, nor things present, nor things to come, nor height, nor depth, nor any other creature, shall be able to separate us from the love of God, which is in Christ Jesus our Lord.

Romans 8:37-39

Thy love to me was wonderful, passing the love of women.

2 Samuel 1:26

Husbands, love your wives, even as Christ also loved the church, and gave himself for it. So ought men to love their wives as their own bodies. He that loveth his wife loveth himself.

Ephesians 5:25, 28

I have loved thee with an everlasting love: therefore with loving-kindness have I drawn thee.

Jeremiah 31:3

His banner over me was love. His left hand is under my head, and his right hand doth embrace me.

Song of Solomon 2:4, 6

Let us consider one another to provoke unto love and to good works.

Hebrews 10:24

It is not good that the man should be alone.

Genesis 2:18

Whoso findeth a wife findeth a good thing, and obtained favor of the Lord.

Proverbs 18:22

Therefore shall a man leave his father and his mother, and shall cleave unto his wife: and they shall be one flesh.

Genesis 2:24

If a kingdom be divided against itself, that kingdom cannot stand. And if a house be divided against itself, that house cannot stand.

Mark 3:24, 25

If a man know not how to rule his own house, how shall he take care of the church of God?

1 Timothy 3:5

By love serve one another.

Galatians 5:13

Better is a dinner of herbs where love is, than a stalled ox and hatred therewith.

Proverbs 15:17

We are members one of another.

Ephesians 4:25

Whither thou goest, I will go; and where thou lodgest, I will lodge: thy people shall be my people, and thy God my God.

Ruth 1:16

Beloved, let us love one another: for love is of God; and every one that loveth is born of God, and knoweth God. He that loveth not, knoweth not God; for God is love. In this was manifested the love of God toward us, because that God sent his only begotten Son into the world, that we might live through him. Herein is love, not that we loved God, but that he loved us, and sent his Son to be the propitiation for our sins.

1 John 4:7–10

What therefore God hath joined together, let no man put asunder.

Matthew 19:6

Beloved, if God so loved us, we ought also to love one another.

1 John 4:11

Hatred stirreth up strifes: but love covereth all sins.

Proverbs 10:12

There is no fear in love; but perfect love casteth out fear: because fear hath torment. He that feareth is not made perfect in love.

1 John 4:18

Jesus went about . . . healing all manner of sickness and all manner of disease among the people. . . . and they brought unto him all sick people that were taken with divers diseases and torments, and those which were possessed with devils, and those which were lunatic, and those that had the palsy; and he healed them.

Matthew 4:23, 24

No man hath seen God at any time. If we love one another, God dwelleth in us, and his love is perfected in us.

1 John 4:12

We have known and believed the love that God hath to us. God is love; and he that dwelleth in love dwelleth in God, and God in him.

1 John 4:16

So then every one of us shall give account of himself to God. Let us not therefore judge one another any more: but judge this rather, that no man put a stumbling block or an occasion to fall in his brother's way.

Romans 14:12, 13

Be kindly affectioned one to another with brotherly love; in honor preferring one another; . . . distributing to the necessity of saints; given to hospitality.

Romans 12:10, 13

And Jesus answering said, A certain man went down from Jerusalem to Jericho, and fell among thieves, which stripped him of his raiment, and wounded him, and departed, leaving him half dead. And by chance there came down a certain priest that way; and when he saw him, he passed by on the other side. And likewise a Levite, when he was at the place, came and looked on him, and passed by on the other side. But a certain Samaritan, as he journeyed, came where he was; and when he saw him, he had compassion on him, and went to him, and bound up his wounds, pouring in oil and wine, and set him on his own beast, and brought him to an inn, and took care of him. Which now of these three, thinkest thou, was neighbor unto him that fell among the thieves? And he said, He that showed mercy on him. Then said Jesus unto him, Go, and do thou likewise.

Luke 10:30−34, 36, 37

―――

Rejoice with them that do rejoice, and weep with them that weep.

Romans 12:15

―――

A friend loveth at all times, and a brother is born for adversity.

Proverbs 17:17

OBEDIENCE

Obedience

Blessed are the undefiled in the way,
who walk in the law of the Lord.
Blessed are they that keep his testimonies,
and that seek him with the whole heart.
Thou hast commanded us
to keep thy precepts diligently.
O that my ways were directed
to keep thy statutes!
Then shall I not be ashamed,
when I have respect unto all thy commandments.
I will praise thee with uprightness of heart,
when I shall have learned thy righteous
   judgments.
I will keep thy statutes:
O forsake me not utterly.

Psalm 119:1, 2, 4–8

Blessed are they that hear the word of God, and keep it.

Luke 11:28

Whatsoever we ask, we receive of him, because we keep his commandments, and do those things that are pleasing in his sight.

1 John 3:22

Go to the ant, thou sluggard; consider her ways, and be wise.

Proverbs 6:6

My son, forget not my law; but let thine heart keep my commandments: for length of days, and long life, and peace, shall they add to thee. Let not mercy and truth forsake thee: bind them about thy neck; write them upon the table of thine heart: so shalt thou find favor and good understanding in the sight of God and man.

Proverbs 3:1—4

Keep the charge of the Lord thy God, to walk in his ways, to keep his statutes, and his commandments, and his judgments, and his testimonies, as it is written in the law of Moses, that thou mayest prosper in all that thou doest, and withersoever thou turnest thyself.

1 Kings 2:3

Then shalt thou prosper, if thou takest heed to fulfil the statutes and judgments which the Lord charged Moses with concerning Israel: be strong, and of good courage; dread not, nor be dismayed.

1 Chronicles 22:13

If they obey and serve him, they shall spend their days in prosperity, and their years in pleasures.

Job 36:11

Herein is my Father glorified, that ye bear much fruit; so shall ye be my disciples. As the Father hath loved me, so have I loved you: continue ye in my love. If ye keep my commandments, ye shall abide in my love; even as I have kept my Father's commandments, and abide in his love. These things have I spoken unto you, that my joy might remain in you, and that your joy might be full.

John 15:8–11

Only be thou strong and very courageous, that thou mayest observe to do according to all the law, which Moses my servant commanded thee: turn not from it to the right hand or to the left, that thou mayest prosper whithersoever thou goest.

Joshua 1:7

I am the vine, ye are the branches. He that abideth in me, and I in him, the same bringeth forth much fruit; for without me ye can do nothing. If ye abide in me, and my words abide in you, ye shall ask what ye will, and it shall be done unto you.

John 15:5, 7

If ye will obey my voice indeed, and keep my covenant, then ye shall be a peculiar treasure unto me above all people: for all the earth is mine.

Exodus 19:5

Trust in the Lord with all thine heart; and lean not unto thine own understanding. In all thy ways acknowledge him, and he shall direct thy paths. Be not wise in thine own eyes: fear the Lord, and depart from evil. It shall be health to thy navel, and marrow to thy bones.

Proverbs 3:5−8

He that hath my commandments, and keepeth them, he it is that loveth me: and he that loveth me shall be loved by my Father, and I will love him, and will manifest myself to him.

John 14:21

If a man keep my saying, he shall never see death.

John 8:51

Hath the Lord as great delight in burnt offerings and sacrifices, as in obeying the voice of the Lord? Behold, to obey is better than sacrifice.

1 Samuel 15:22

Jesus answered and said unto him, If a man love me, he will keep my words: and my Father will love him, and we will come unto him, and make our abode with him.

John 14:23

Except the Lord build the house,
they labor in vain that build it:
except the Lord keep the city,
the watchman waketh but in vain.

Psalm 127:1

My foot hath held his steps, his way have I kept, and not declined. Neither have I gone back from the commandment of his lips; I have esteemed the words of his mouth more than my necessary food.

Job 23:11, 12

Blessed are they that do his commandments, that they may have right to the tree of life, and may enter in through the gates into the city.

Revelation 22:14

Lord, now lettest thou thy servant depart in peace, according to thy word.

Luke 2:29

PRAISE
PROTECTION

Praise

It is a good thing to give thanks
  unto the Lord,
and to sing praises unto thy name,
  O Most High:
to show forth thy loving-kindness in
  the morning,
and thy faithfulness every night,
upon an instrument of ten strings,
  and upon the psaltery;
upon the harp with a solemn sound.

Psalm 92:1−3

While I live will I praise the Lord:
I will sing praises unto my God while I have
  any being.

Psalm 146:2

I will open my mouth in a parable:
I will utter dark sayings of old:
which we have heard and known,
and our fathers have told us.
We will not hide them from their children,
showing to the generation to come
the praises of the Lord, and his strength,
and his wonderful works that he hath done.

Psalm 78:2−4

225

O Lord my God, thou art very great;
thou art clothed with honor and majesty:
who coverest thyself with light as
   with a garment:
who stretchest out the heavens like a curtain:
who layeth the beams of his chambers
   in the waters:
who maketh the clouds his chariot:
who walketh upon the wings of the wind:
who maketh his angels spirits;
his ministers a flaming fire.

Psalm 104:1—4

Ye are the light of the world. A city that is set on a hill cannot be hid. Neither do men light a candle, and put it under a bushel, but on a candlestick; and it giveth light unto all that are in the house. Let your light so shine before men, that they may see your good works, and glorify your Father which is in heaven.

Matthew 5:14—16

Thou shalt rejoice in every good thing which the Lord thy God hath given unto thee, and unto thine house.

Deuteronomy 26:11

O Lord, I will praise thee: though thou wast angry with me, thine anger is turned away, and thou comfortedst me. Behold, God is my salvation; I will trust, and not be afraid: for the Lord Jehovah is my strength and my song; he also is become my salvation. Therefore with joy shall ye draw water out of the wells of salvation.

Isaiah 12:1−3

Why art thou cast down, O my soul?
And why art thou disquieted within me?
Hope thou in God: for I shall yet praise him,
who is the health of my countenance,
   and my God.

Psalm 42:11

Thou shalt fear the Lord thy God; him shalt thou serve, and to him shalt thou cleave, and swear by his name. He is thy praise, and he is thy God.

Deuteronomy 10:20, 21

Rejoice evermore. Pray without ceasing. In every thing give thanks: for this is the will of God in Christ Jesus concerning you.

1 Thessalonians 5:16−18

A man hath joy by the answer of his mouth: and a word spoken in due season, how good is it!

Proverbs 15:23

My soul doth magnify the Lord, and my spirit hath rejoiced in God my Saviour. For he hath regarded the low estate of his handmaiden: for, behold, from henceforth all generations shall call me blessed. For he that is mighty hath done to me great things; and holy is his name. And his mercy is on them that fear him from generation to generation. He hath showed strength with his arm; he hath scattered the proud in the imagination of their hearts. He hath put down the mighty from their seats, and exalted them of low degree. He hath filled the hungry with good things; and the rich he hath sent empty away. He hath holpen his servant Israel, in remembrance of his mercy; as he spake to our fathers, to Abraham, and to his seed for ever.

Luke 1:46—55

Thy mercy, O Lord, is in the heavens;
and thy faithfulness reacheth unto the
 clouds.
Thy righteousness is like the great mountains;
thy judgments are a great deep:
O Lord, thou preservest man and beast.

How excellent is thy loving-kindness, O God!

Psalm 36:5—7

Now unto him that is able to do exceeding abundantly above all that we ask or think, according to the power that worketh within us, unto him be glory in the church by Christ Jesus throughout all ages, world without end.

Ephesians 3:20, 21

Protection

The Lord is my light and my salvation;
whom shall I fear?
The Lord is the strength of my life;
of whom shall I be afraid?

When the wicked, even mine enemies and my foes,
came upon me to eat up my flesh,
they stumbled and fell.

Though a host should encamp against me,
my heart shall not fear:
though war should rise against me,
in this will I be confident.

Psalm 27:1–3

It is God that girdeth me with strength,
and maketh my way perfect.

Psalm 18:32

For the Lord your God is he that goeth with you, to fight for
you against your enemies, to save you.

Deuteronomy 20:4

The joy of the Lord is your strength.

Nehemiah 8:10

For the Lord God is a sun and shield:
the Lord will give grace and glory:
no good thing will he withhold from them
    that walk uprightly.

Psalm 84:11

The Lord shall preserve thee from all evil:
he shall preserve thy soul.
The Lord shall preserve thy going out
    and thy coming in
from this time forth, and even for evermore.

Psalm 121:7, 8

A man's heart deviseth his way: but the Lord directeth his
steps.

Proverbs 16:9

He shall cover thee with his feathers,
and under his wings shalt thou trust:
his truth shall be thy shield and buckler.

Psalm 91:4

The beloved of the Lord shall dwell in safety by him; and the
Lord shall cover him all the day long.

Deuteronomy 33:12

When thou passeth through the waters, I will be with thee; and through the rivers, they shall not overflow thee: when thou walkest through the fire, thou shalt not be burned; neither shall the flame kindle upon thee.

Isaiah 43:2

―――

Fear thou not; for I am with thee: be not dismayed; for I am thy God: I will strengthen thee; yea, I will help thee; yea, I will uphold thee with the right hand of my righteousness.

Isaiah 41:10

―――

For I the Lord thy God will hold thy right hand, saying unto thee, Fear not; I will help thee.

Isaiah 41:13

―――

Whoso hearkeneth unto me shall dwell safely, and shall be quiet from fear of evil.

Proverbs 1:33

―――

Think not that I am come to destroy the law, or the prophets: I am not come to destroy, but to fulfil. For verily I say unto you, Till heaven and earth pass, one jot or one tittle shall in no wise pass from the law, till all be fulfilled.

Matthew 5:17, 18

Though I walk in the midst of trouble,
   thou wilt revive me:
thou shalt stretch forth thine hand
   against the wrath of mine enemies,
and thy right hand shall save me.

Psalm 138:7

(The Lord thy God is a merciful God;) he will not forsake
thee, neither destroy thee, nor forget the covenant of thy
fathers, which he sware unto them.

Deuteronomy 4:31

He shall send from heaven, and save me
from the reproach of him that would
   swallow me up.
God shall send forth his mercy and his truth.

Psalm 57:3

We may boldly say, The Lord is my helper, and I will not fear
what man shall do unto me.

Hebrews 13:6

Hearken unto me, ye that know righteousness, the people in
whose heart is my law; fear ye not the reproach of men,
neither be ye afraid of their revilings.

Isaiah 51:7

The Lord also will be a refuge for
the oppressed,
a refuge in times of trouble.
And they that know thy name will put
their trust in thee:
for thou, Lord, hast not forsaken them
that seek thee.

Psalm 9:9, 10

If God be for us, who can be against us?

Romans 8:31

The name of the Lord is a strong tower: the righteous runneth
into it, and is safe.

Proverbs 18:10

In the fear of the Lord is strong confidence: and his children
shall have a place of refuge.

Proverbs 14:26

God is our refuge and strength,
a very present help in trouble.

Psalm 46:1

The eternal God is thy refuge, and underneath are the everlasting arms.

Deuteronomy 33:27

Thou art my hiding place;
thou shalt preserve me from trouble;
thou shalt compass me about with songs
    of deliverance.

Psalm 32:7

I will say of the Lord,
He is my refuge and my fortress:
my God; in him will I trust.

Psalm 91:2

Thou hast been a strength to the poor, a strength to the needy
in his stress, a refuge from the storm, a shadow from the heat.

Isaiah 25:4

Thou has been a shelter for me,
and a strong tower from the enemy.

Psalm 61:3

I will both lay me down in peace,
    and sleep:
for thou, Lord, only makest me
    dwell in safety.

Psalm 4:8

R

REWARD

Reward

Blessed are they which are persecuted for righteousness' sake: for theirs is the kingdom of heaven. Blessed are ye, when men shall revile you, and persecute you, and shall say all manner of evil against you falsely, for my sake. Rejoice, and be exceeding glad: for great is your reward in heaven: for so persecuted they the prophets which were before you.

Matthew 5:10−12

Seek not ye what ye shall eat, or what ye shall drink, neither be ye of doubtful mind. For all these things do the nations of the world seek after: and your Father knoweth that ye have need of these things. But rather seek ye the kingdom of God; and all these things shall be added unto you.

Luke 12:29−31

If ye then, being evil, know how to give good gifts unto your children, how much more shall your Father which is in heaven give good things to them that ask him?

Matthew 7:11

Eye hath not seen, nor ear heard, neither have entered into the heart of man, the things which God hath prepared for them that love him.

1 Corinthians 2:9

To him that overcometh will I give to eat of the hidden manna, and will give him a white stone, and in the stone a new name written, which no man knoweth saving he that receiveth it.

Revelation 2:17

———

As long as he sought the Lord, God made him to prosper.

2 Chronicles 26:5

———

Be thou faithful unto death, and I will give thee a crown of life.

Revelation 2:10

———

I am the bread of life: he that cometh to me shall never hunger; and he that believeth on me shall never thirst.

John 6:35

———

He which soweth sparingly shall reap also sparingly; and he which soweth bountifully shall reap also bountifully.

2 Corinthians 9:6

———

To him that soweth righteousness shall be a sure reward.

Proverbs 11:18

———

He that is least among you all, the same shall be great.

Luke 9:48

Blessed is every one that feareth the Lord;
that walketh in his ways.
For thou shalt eat the labor of thine hands:
happy shalt thou be,
and it shall be well with thee.

Thy wife shall be as a fruitful vine
by the sides of thine house:
thy children like olive plants
round about thy table.
Behold, that thus shall the man be blessed that
    feareth the Lord.

Psalm 128:1−4

A new heart also will I give you, and a new spirit will I put within you: and I will take away the stony heart out of your flesh, and I will give you a heart of flesh.

Ezekiel 36:26

God is able to make all grace abound toward you; that ye, always having all sufficiency in all things, may abound to every good work.

2 Corinthians 9:8

The Lord shall increase you more and more,
you and your children.

Psalm 115:14

Is not this the fast that I have chosen? to loose the bands of wickedness, to undo the heavy burdens, and to let the oppressed go free, and that ye break every yoke? Is it not to deal thy bread to the hungry, and that thou bring the poor that are cast out to thy house? when thou seest the naked, that thou cover him; and that thou hide not thyself from thine own flesh? Then shall thy light break forth as the morning, and thine health shall spring forth speedily: and thy righteousness shall go before thee; the glory of the Lord shall be thy reward.

Isaiah 58:6−8

The Lord rewarded me according to my righteousness; according to the cleanness of my hands hath he recompensed me.

2 Samuel 22:21

For God giveth to a man that is good in his sight, wisdom, and knowledge, and joy.

Ecclesiastes 2:26

I bow my knees unto the Father of our Lord Jesus Christ, of whom the whole family in heaven and earth is named, that he would grant you, according to the riches of his glory, to be strengthened with might by his Spirit in the inner man; that Christ may dwell in your hearts by faith; that ye, being rooted and grounded in love, may be able to comprehend with all saints what is the breadth, and length, and depth, and height; and to know the love of Christ, which passeth knowledge, that ye might be filled with all the fulness of God.

Ephesians 3:14−19

Be not deceived; God is not mocked: for whatsoever a man soweth, that shall he also reap. For he that soweth to his flesh shall of the flesh reap corruption; but he that soweth to the Spirit shall of the Spirit reap life everlasting. And let us not be weary in well doing: for in due season we shall reap, if we faint not. As we have therefore opportunity, let us do good unto all men.

Galatians 6:7–10

I have been young, and now am old;
yet have I not seen the righteous forsaken,
nor his seed begging bread.

Psalm 37:25

And we know that all things work together for good to them that love God, to them who are the called according to his purpose.

Romans 8:28

Lay not up for yourselves treasures upon earth, where moth and rust doth corrupt, and where thieves break through and steal: but lay up for yourselves treasures in heaven, where neither moth nor rust doth corrupt, and where thieves do not break through nor steal: for where your treasure is, there will your heart be also.

Matthew 6:19–21

241

No man can serve two masters: for either he will hate the one, and love the other; or else he will hold to the one, and despise the other. Ye cannot serve God and mammon. Therefore I say unto you, Take no thought for your life, what ye shall eat, or what ye shall drink; nor yet for your body, what ye shall put on. Is not the life more than meat, and the body than raiment? Behold the fowls of the air: for they sow not, neither do they reap, nor gather into barns; yet your heavenly Father feedeth them. Are ye not much better than they?

Matthew 6:24−26

What is a man profited, if he shall gain the whole world, and lose his own soul? or what shall a man give in exchange for his soul? For the Son of man shall come in the glory of his Father with his angels; and then he shall reward every man according to his works.

Matthew 16:26, 27

He that followeth after righteousness and mercy findeth life, righteousness, and honor.

Proverbs 21:21

Godliness is profitable unto all things, having promise of the life that now is, and of that which is to come.

1 Timothy 4:8

The fruit of the Spirit is love, joy, peace, long-suffering, gentleness, goodness, faith, meekness, temperance.

Galatians 5:22, 23

Behold that which I have seen: it is good and comely for one to eat and to drink, and to enjoy the good of all his labor that he taketh under the sun all the days of his life, which God giveth him: for it is his portion.

Ecclesiastes 5:18

A merry heart maketh a cheerful countenance.

Proverbs 15:13

He that is of a merry heart hath a continual feast.

Proverbs 15:15

Thou wilt keep him in perfect peace, whose mind is stayed on thee: because he trusteth in thee.

Isaiah 26:3

There remaineth therefore a rest to the people of God. For he that is entered into his rest, he also hath ceased from his own works, as God did from his. Let us labor therefore to enter into that rest.

Hebrews 4:9, 10

For, lo, the winter is past, the rain is over and gone; the flowers appear on the earth; the time of the singing of birds is come, and the voice of the turtle is heard in our land.

Song of Solomon 2:11, 12

S

SACRIFICE

Sacrifice

There are three things that are never satisfied, yea, four things say not, It is enough: the grave; and the barren womb; the earth that is not filled with water; and the fire that saith not, It is enough.

Proverbs 30:15, 16

Bear ye one another's burdens, and so fulfil the law of Christ.

Galatians 6:2

We then that are strong ought to bear the infirmities of the weak, and not to please ourselves.

Romans 15:1

Who is he that will harm you, if ye be followers of that which is good? But and if ye suffer for righteousness' sake, happy are ye.

1 Peter 3:13, 14

The sufferings of this present time are not worthy to be compared with the glory which shall be revealed in us.

Romans 8:18

We are troubled on every side, yet not distressed; we are perplexed, but not in despair; persecuted, but not forsaken; cast down, but not destroyed; always bearing about in the body the dying of the Lord Jesus, that the life also of Jesus might be made manifest in our body.

2 Corinthians 4:8−10

But the God of all grace, who hath called us unto his eternal glory by Christ Jesus, after that ye have suffered a while, make you perfect, stablish, strengthen, settle you.

1 Peter 5:10

Many are the afflictions of the righteous:
but the Lord delivereth him out of them all.

Psalm 34:19

He that loveth silver shall not be satisfied with silver; nor he that loveth abundance with increase: this is also vanity. The sleep of a laboring man is sweet, whether he eat little or much: but the abundance of the rich will not suffer him to sleep.

Ecclesiastes 5:10,12

The world cannot hate you; but me it hateth, because I testify of it, that the works thereof are evil.

John 7:7

Beloved, think it not strange concerning the fiery trial which is to try you, as though some strange thing happened unto you: but rejoice, inasmuch as ye are partakers of Christ's sufferings; that, when his glory shall be revealed, ye may be glad also with exceeding joy. If ye be reproached for the name of Christ, happy are ye; for the Spirit of glory and of God resteth upon you. . . . Yet if any man suffer as a Christian, let him not be ashamed; but let him glorify God on this behalf.

1 Peter 4:12-14,16

It is better to go to the house of mourning, than to go to the house of feasting.

Ecclesiastes 7:2

If, when ye do well, and suffer for it, ye take it patiently, this is acceptable with God. For even hereunto were ye called: because Christ also suffered for us, leaving us an example, that ye should follow his steps.

1 Peter 2:20, 21

He said unto me, My grace is sufficient for thee: for my strength is made perfect in weakness. Most gladly therefore will I rather glory in my infirmities, that the power of Christ may rest upon me. Therefore I take pleasure in infirmities, . . . for Christ's sake: for when I am weak, then am I strong.

2 Corinthians 12:9, 10

He said to them all, If any man will come after me, let him deny himself, and take up his cross daily, and follow me. For whosoever will save his life shall lose it: but whosoever will lose his life for my sake, the same shall save it.

Luke 9:23, 24

━━━━━

God forbid that I should glory, save in the cross of our Lord Jesus Christ, by whom the world is crucified unto me, and I unto the world.

Galatians 6:14

━━━━━

Ye shall be hated by all men for my name's sake: but he that endureth to the end shall be saved.

Matthew 10:22

━━━━━

But we see Jesus, who was made a little lower than the angels for the suffering of death, crowned with glory and honor; that he by the grace of God should taste death for every man.

Hebrews 2:9

━━━━━

As ye are partakers of the sufferings, so shall ye be also of the consolation.

2 Corinthians 1:7

I say unto you, That ye shall weep and lament, but the world shall rejoice; and ye shall be sorrowful, but your sorrow shall be turned into joy. A woman when she is in travail hath sorrow, because her hour is come: but as soon as she is delivered of the child, she remembereth no more the anguish, for joy that a man is born into the world. And ye now therefore have sorrow: but I will see you again, and your heart shall rejoice, and your joy no man taketh from you. And in that day ye shall ask me nothing. Verily, verily, I say unto you, Whatsoever ye shall ask the Father in my name, he will give it to you. Hitherto have ye asked nothing in my name: ask, and ye shall receive, that your joy may be full.

John 16:20−24

I beseech you therefore, brethren, by the mercies of God, that ye present your bodies a living sacrifice, holy, acceptable unto God, which is your reasonable service.

Romans 12:1

[Jesus said,] I am come that they might have life, and that they might have it more abundantly.

John 10:10

Whosoever will be great among you, shall be your minister: and whosoever of you will be the chiefest, shall be servant of all. For even the Son of man came not to be ministered unto, but to minister, and to give his life a ransom for many.

Mark 10:43−45

Ye know the grace of our Lord Jesus Christ, that, though he was rich, yet for your sakes he became poor, that ye through his poverty might be rich.

2 Corinthians 8:9

The foxes have holes, and the birds of the air have nests; but the Son of man hath not where to lay his head.

Matthew 8:20

[He] bare our sins in his own body on the tree, that we, being dead to sins, should live unto righteousness: by whose stripes ye were healed.

1 Peter 2:24

Yet a little while, and the world seeth me no more; but ye see me: because I live, ye shall live also.

John 14:19

For the Son of man is come to seek and to save that which was lost.

Luke 19:10

T

TEMPTATION

Temptation

There hath no temptation taken you but such as is common to man: but God is faithful, who will not suffer you to be tempted above that ye are able; but will with the temptation also make a way to escape, that ye may be able to bear it.

1 Corinthians 10:13

Blessed is the man that endureth temptation: for when he is tried, he shall receive the crown of life, which the Lord hath promised to them that love him.

James 1:12

For in that he himself hath suffered being tempted, he is able to succor them that are tempted.

Hebrews 2:18

Because thou hast kept the word of my patience, I also will keep thee from the hour of temptation, which shall come upon all the world, to try them that dwell upon the earth.

Revelation 3:10

If iniquity be in thine hand, put it far away, and let not wickedness dwell in thy tabernacles. For then shalt thou lift up thy face without spot; yea, thou shalt be steadfast, and shalt not fear.

Job 11:14, 15

Whoso shall offend one of these little ones which believe in me, it were better for him that a millstone were hanged about his neck, and that he were drowned in the depth of the sea. Woe unto the world because of offenses! for it must needs be that offenses come; but woe to that man by whom the offense cometh! Wherefore if thy hand or thy foot offend thee, cut them off, and cast them from thee: it is better for thee to enter into life halt or maimed, rather than having two hands or two feet to be cast into everlasting fire. And if thine eye offend thee, pluck it out, and cast it from thee: it is better for thee to enter into life with one eye, rather than having two eyes to be cast into hell fire.

Matthew 18:6−9

Enter ye in at the strait gate: for wide is the gate, and broad is the way, that leadeth to destruction, and many there be which go in thereat: because strait is the gate, and narrow is the way, which leadeth unto life, and few there be that find it.

Matthew 7:13, 14

Watch ye and pray, lest ye enter into temptation. The spirit truly is ready, but the flesh is weak.

Mark 14:38

He that overcometh, the same shall be clothed in white raiment; and I will not blot out his name out of the book of life, but I will confess his name before my Father, and before his angels.

Revelation 3:5

256

To keep thee from the evil woman, from the flattery of the tongue of a strange woman. Lust not after her beauty in thine heart; neither let her take thee with her eyelids. For by means of a whorish woman a man is brought to a piece of bread: and the adulteress will hunt for the precious life. Can a man take fire in his bosom, and his clothes not be burned? Can one go upon hot coals, and his feet not be burned? So he that goeth in to his neighbor's wife; whosoever toucheth her shall not be innocent.

Proverbs 6:24−29

Whosoever looketh on a woman to lust after her hath committed adultery with her already in his heart.

Matthew 5:28

Man is born unto trouble, as the sparks fly upward.

Job 5:7

Put not your trust in princes.

Psalm 146:3

Beware of false prophets, which come to you in sheep's clothing, but inwardly they are ravening wolves.

Matthew 7:15

I say unto you, Swear not at all.

Matthew 5:34

We know that whosoever is born of God sinneth not; but he that is begotten of God keepeth himself, and that wicked one toucheth him not.

1 John 5:18

Be sober, be vigilant; because your adversary the devil, as a roaring lion, walketh about, seeking whom he may devour.

1 Peter 5:8

Take heed, brethren, lest there be in any of you an evil heart of unbelief, in departing from the living God.

Hebrews 3:12

The heart is deceitful above all things, and desperately wicked: who can know it?

Jeremiah 17:9

This only have I found, that God hath made man upright; but they have sought out many inventions.

Ecclesiastes 7:29

The good that I would, I do not: but the evil which I would not, that I do.

Romans 7:19

Get thee behind me, Satan.

Matthew 16:23

There be three things which are too wonderful for me, yea, four which I know not: the way of an eagle in the air; the way of a serpent upon a rock; the way of a ship in the midst of the sea; and the way of a man with a maid.

Proverbs 30:18, 19

The love of money is the root of all evil.

1 Timothy 6:10

He that walketh with wise men shall be wise: but a companion of fools shall be destroyed.

Proverbs 13:20

Fret not thyself because of evil men, neither be thou envious at the wicked.

Proverbs 24:19

Fear not them which kill the body, but are not able to kill the soul: but rather fear him which is able to destroy both soul and body in hell.

Matthew 10:28

My brethren, count it all joy when ye fall into divers temptations; knowing this, that the trying of your faith worketh patience.

James 1:2, 3

V

VIRTUE AND VICE

Virtue and Vice

Wherefore God also gave them up to uncleanness, through the lusts of their own hearts, to dishonor their own bodies between themselves: who changed the truth of God into a lie, and worshipped and served the creature more than the Creator, who is blessed for ever.

Romans 1:24, 25

Blessed is the man that walketh not
  in the counsel of the ungodly,
nor standeth in the way of sinners,
nor sitteth in the seat of the scornful.

Psalm 1:1

Where envying and strife is, there is confusion and every evil work.

James 3:16

What doth the Lord require of thee, but to do justly, and to love mercy, and to walk humbly with thy God?

Micah 6:8

Such as are upright in their way are his delight.

Proverbs 11:20

Let me die the death of the righteous. . . .

Numbers 23:10

Who can find a virtuous woman? For her price is far above rubies. The heart of her husband doth safely trust in her, so that he shall have no need of spoil. She will do him good and not evil all the days of her life. . . . She openeth her mouth with wisdom; and in her tongue is the law of kindness. She looketh well to the ways of her household, and eateth not the bread of idleness. . . . Favor is deceitful, and beauty is vain: but a woman that feareth the Lord, she shall be praised. Give her of the fruit of her hands; and let her own works praise her in the gates.

Proverbs 31:10−12,26,27,30,31

Whatsoever thy hand findeth to do, do it with thy might.

Ecclesiastes 9:10

A good name is better than precious ointment.

Ecclesiastes 7:1

He that diggeth a pit shall fall into it.

Ecclesiastes 10:8

Let no man despise thy youth; but be thou an example of the believers, in word, in conversation, in charity, in faith, in purity.

1 Timothy 4:12

A good name is rather to be chosen than great riches, and loving favor rather than silver and gold.

Proverbs 22:1

Finally, brothers, whatsoever things are true, whatsoever things are honest, whatsoever things are just, whatsoever things are pure, whatsoever things are lovely, whatsoever things are of good report; if there be any virtue, and if there be any praise, think on these things. Those things, which ye have both learned, and received, and heard, and seen in me, do: and the God of peace shall be with you.

Philippians 4:8−9

The just man walketh in his integrity: his children are blessed after him.

Proverbs 20:7

Whosoever shall keep the whole law, and yet offend in one point, he is guilty of all.

James 2:10

Wine is a mocker, strong drink is raging.

Proverbs 20:1

The night is far spent, the day is at hand: let us therefore cast off the works of darkness, and let us put on the armor of light. Let us walk honestly, as in the day; not in rioting and drunkenness, not in chambering and wantonness, not in strife and envying: but put ye on the Lord Jesus Christ, and make not provision for the flesh, to fulfil the lusts thereof.

Romans 13:12−14

Unto the upright there ariseth light
   in the darkness:
he is gracious, and full of compassion,
   and righteous.
A good man showeth favor, and lendeth:
he will guide his affairs with discretion.
Surely he shall not be moved for ever:
the righteous shall be in everlasting
   remembrance.
He hath dispersed,
he hath given to the poor;
his righteousness endureth for ever;
his horn shall be exalted with honor.

Psalm 112:4−6, 9

The eyes of the Lord are upon the righteous,
and his ears are open to their cry.

Psalm 34:15

The wicked borroweth, and payeth not again:
but the righteous showeth mercy, and giveth.
For such as be blessed of him shall inherit the earth;
and they that be cursed of him shall be cut off.

Psalm 37:21, 22

For thou, Lord, wilt bless the
   righteous;
with favor wilt thou compass him as
   with a shield.

Psalm 5:12

WORSHIP

Worship

If any man among you seem to be religious, and bridleth not his tongue, but deceiveth his own heart, this man's religion is vain. Pure religion and undefiled before God and Father is this, To visit the fatherless and widows in their affliction, and to keep himself unspotted from the world.

James 1:26, 27

Thus saith the Lord, The heaven is my throne, and the earth is my footstool: where is the house that ye build unto me? and where is the place of my rest?

Isaiah 66:1

God is a Spirit: and they that worship him must worship him in spirit and in truth.

John 4:24

Again I say unto you, That if two of you shall agree on earth as touching any thing that they shall ask, it shall be done for them of my Father which is in heaven. For where two or three are gathered together in my name, there am I in the midst of them.

Matthew 18:19, 20

When he had called all the people unto him, he said unto them, Hearken unto me every one of you, and understand: there is nothing from without a man, that entering into him can defile him: but the things which come out of him, those are they that defile the man. For from within, out of the heart of men, proceed evil thoughts, adulteries, fornications, murders, thefts, covetousness, wickedness, deceit, lasciviousness, an evil eye, blasphemy, pride, foolishness: all these evil things come from within, and defile the man.

Mark 7:14–15, 21–23

I desired mercy, and not sacrifice; and the knowledge of God more than burnt offerings.

Hosea 6:6

Better is a dry morsel, and quietness therewith, than a house full of sacrifices with strife.

Proverbs 17:1

Whose adorning, let it not be that outward adorning of plaiting the hair, and of wearing of gold, or of putting on of apparel; but let it be the hidden man of the heart, in that which is not corruptible, even the ornament of a meek and quiet spirit, which is in the sight of God of great price.

1 Peter 3:3, 4

Then Paul stood in the midst of Mars' hill, and said, Ye men of Athens, I perceive that in all things ye are too superstitious. For as I passed by, and beheld your devotions, I found an altar with this inscription, TO THE UNKNOWN GOD. Whom therefore ye ignorantly worship, him declare I unto you. God that made the world and all things therein, seeing that he is Lord of heaven and earth, dwelleth not in temples made with hands; neither is worshipped with men's hands, as though he needed any thing, seeing he giveth to all life, and breath, and all things; and hath made of one blood all nations of men for to dwell on all the face of the earth, and hath determined the times before appointed, and the bounds of their habitation; that they should seek the Lord, if haply they might feel after him, and find him, though he be not far from every one of us: for in him we live, and move, and have our being; as certain also of your own poets have said, For we are also his offspring.

Acts 17:22−28

And the scribe said unto him, Well, Master, thou hast said the truth: for there is one God; and there is none other but he: and love him with all the heart, and with all the understanding, and with all the soul, and with all the strength, and to love his neighbor as himself, is more than all whole burnt offerings and sacrifices.

Mark 12:32, 33

Know thou the God of thy father, and serve him with a perfect heart and with a willing mind: for the Lord searchest all hearts, and understandest all the imaginations of the thoughts: if thou seek him, he will be found of thee.

1 Chronicles 28:9

This one thing I do, forgetting those things which are behind, and reaching forth unto those things which are before, I press toward the mark for the prize of the high calling of God in Christ Jesus.

Philippians 3:13, 14

The Lord direct your hearts into the love of God, and into the patient waiting for Christ.

2 Thessalonians 3:5

The sacrifice of the wicked is an abomination to the Lord: but the prayer of the upright is his delight.

Proverbs 15:8

Let us search and try our ways, and turn again to the Lord. Let us lift up our heart with our hands unto God in the heavens.

Lamentations 3:40, 41

Seek ye the Lord while he may be found, call ye upon him while he is near.

Isaiah 55:6

But if from thence thou shalt seek the Lord thy God, thou shalt find him, if thou seek him with all thy heart and with all thy soul.

Deuteronomy 4:29

Let the words of my mouth, and the
    meditation of my heart,
be acceptable in thy sight,
O God, my strength, and my redeemer.

Psalm 19:14

I have set the Lord always before me:
because he is at my right hand, I shall
    not be moved.

Psalm 16:8

My soul thirsteth for God, for the
    living God:
when shall I come and appear before God?

Psalm 42:2

)